When the Gromulans kidnap the Galactic President and hide him somewhere on planet Earth, the powers that be naturally turn to you: for YOU are the top Rogue Tracer of the sector where this minor planet is situated. Your job is to rescue him. You do not know where he is, but you know that you will be up against cunning opponents and some of the deadliest Androids in the galaxy . . . and you are well aware that there are likely to be many unforeseen dangers as well. You have only forty-eight hours in which to succeed; after that, the brainscanning of the President will be complete . . .

Two dice, a pencil and an eraser are all you need to embark on this thrilling adventure, which is complete with its elaborate combat system and a score sheet to record your gains and losses.

Many dangers lie ahead and your success is by no means certain. YOU decide which routes to follow, which dangers to risk and which adversaries to fight!

Fighting Fantasy Gamebooks

1. THE WARLOCK OF FIRETOP MOUNTAIN
2. THE CITADEL OF CHAOS
3. THE FOREST OF DOOM
4. STARSHIP TRAVELLER
5. CITY OF THIEVES
6. DEATHTRAP DUNGEON
7. ISLAND OF THE LIZARD KING
8. SCORPION SWAMP
9. CAVERNS OF THE SNOW WITCH
10. HOUSE OF HELL
11. TALISMAN OF DEATH
12. SPACE ASSASSIN
13. FREEWAY FIGHTER
14. TEMPLE OF TERROR
15. THE RINGS OF KETHER
16. SEAS OF BLOOD
17. APPOINTMENT WITH F.E.A.R.
18. REBEL PLANET
19. DEMONS OF THE DEEP
20. SWORD OF THE SAMURAI
21. TRIAL OF CHAMPIONS
22. ROBOT COMMANDO
23. MASKS OF MAYHEM
24. CREATURE OF HAVOC
25. BENEATH NIGHTMARE CASTLE
26. CRYPT OF THE SORCERER

Steve Jackson's SORCERY!
1. The Shamutanti Hills
2. Kharé – Cityport of Traps
3. The Seven Serpents
4. The Crown of Kings

FIGHTING FANTASY – The Role-playing Game
THE RIDDLING REAVER
OUT OF THE PIT – Fighting Fantasy Monsters
TITAN – The Fighting Fantasy World

Steve Jackson and Ian Livingstone
present:

Star Strider

Luke Sharp

Illustrated by Gary Mayes

PUFFIN BOOKS

Puffin Books, Penguin Books Ltd, Harmondsworth, Middlesex, England
Viking Penguin Inc., 40 West 23rd Street, New York, New York 10010, U.S.A.
Penguin Books Australia Ltd, Ringwood, Victoria, Australia
Penguin Books Canada Ltd, 2801 John Street, Markham, Ontario, Canada L3R 1B4
Penguin Books (N.Z.) Ltd, 182–190 Wairau Road, Auckland 10, New Zealand

First published 1987
Reprinted 1987

Concept copyright © Steve Jackson and Ian Livingstone, 1987
Text copyright © Luke Sharp, 1987
Illustrations copyright © Gary Mayes, 1987
All rights reserved

Printed and bound in Great Britain by
Cox & Wyman Ltd, Reading
Set in 11/13 pt Linotron Palatino by
Rowland Phototypesetting Ltd
Bury St Edmunds, Suffolk

Except in the United States of America,
this book is sold subject to the condition
that it shall not, by way of trade or otherwise,
be lent, re-sold, hired out, or otherwise circulated
without the publisher's prior consent in any form of
binding or cover other than that in which it is
published and without a similar condition
including this condition being imposed
on the subsequent purchaser

*To Isabelle
and the Felines from Wistas 4*

CONTENTS

THE MISSION
9

LIKELY ENEMIES
12

WEAPONS
15

ABILITIES
16

COMBAT
19

FEATS AND TASKS
21

ADVENTURE SHEET
22

STAR STRIDER
25

THE MISSION

Rogue Tracer. A hunter of fugitives, criminals and wanted beings who have a price on their heads. Formerly known as bounty hunters. Licensed by the Tracebeam Organization. Elite Rogue Tracers are known as Star Striders.
Encyclopedia Galactica

Special message follows . . .

The Gromulans have kidnapped President Xerin of Galaxy One Federation. He has been taken to a quadrant in the northern hemisphere of the planet Earth. It is feared that he is being brainscanned at this very moment and the Zand Corporation assures us that his cephaloprotector will hold out only for a further forty-eight gravity hours. After that time our computer defence codes will be in Gromulan hands and probably in the hands of our enemies, the Empire of the Purple Flag. You are the best Rogue Tracer in Sector 6. In the galactic top money-making table, you rank 97. You have been chosen very carefully and your mission, should you decide to accept it (Standard Contract, M.I., Special Rates), is as follows:

You will make your way to Earth under the pretext of your Rogue Tracer activities, locate the President and GET HIM OUT. Spacefleet 7 will be waiting in

Earth orbit for your signal. Please note that successful completion of your mission will make you very rich, but if you do not accept the assignment, Tracebeam assure us that they cannot guarantee the future flow of criminal records to your terminal for tracing.

Please indicate your acceptance of the mission (Y/N) . . .

Thank you. Further details now follow:

The Gromulans are a humanoid, hyper-intelligent people of unknown origin who have previously only dabbled in world-scale terrorism. They are experts in the construction of Androids and are masters of illusion. They are the originators of Illus-o-Vision 70 for Galaxy Ents Corporation, but were robbed of all copyright in the last century. Their latest invention is the Illus-o-Scope, a portable illusion generator. The Gromulans will be expecting a rescue attempt, so BEWARE! To assist you, we are activating our 'planted' spy Androids in that sector. Look out for these and the CodeMatch signal, but be extremely careful: the Groms are experts in 'turning' dedicated Androids.

The Gromulans have been using Earth as a base for the last century. It is a small, insignificant planet on the edge of the galaxy. Once heavily populated, but now in decline, most of its native inhabitants have emigrated to Alphacent. Its only source of credits is the servicing of freightcruisers and the mining of salt. Unfortunately, the phozon crystal does not function in that solar system and we cannot pinpoint locations with sensormatics. You will have to signal the rescue fleet once you have found the President.

The remoteness of the Earth and the lack of sensor detection has meant that fugitives have flocked to the planet. You will find many 'targets' on Earth, so you may be kept busy in your normal profession; this makes the rescue more difficult, but also strengthens your cover.

LIKELY ENEMIES

Gromulans

Gromulans are very intelligent humanoids, who would rather surrender than risk a fight in the physical sense. They specialize in deception and can talk the three hind legs off a Wooki. They were nomadic, but have settled on Earth for the last hundred gravity years, where they have developed their Androids and patent Illus-o-Scope. Some reports talk of an addiction to chess and small Earth snails.

Gromulan Androids

These can vary tremendously in design and type. They are the main power-base of the Groms and the Excel Class are VERY DANGEROUS. You are skilled in techniques of fighting Androids and will have a good chance against Guards, GromPols, Admins, Sweepertrons, etc., but try to steer clear of Excels. If you do get close to one, probe for de-activation points: the Groms fear their creations turning on them and all models have built-in weak spots. As with all standard types, a badly damaged Android will self-destruct.

Fugitives and Criminals

You may meet anyone from a tax-dodging Ferian to a Pirate Prince. Many will leave you alone, but if they suspect you of being a Rogue Tracer, they may run or attack. Remember, you operate within the Galactic Law and are bound not to kill human beings. If you do, you will be a fugitive and be hunted down. If you do trace fugitives, 'cache and mark' them for future collection.

Houlgans

These are local feuding groups of native Earth origin, believed to number 80–90 tribes. They base their fanaticism on some long-forgotten religion, which revolves around colours of clothing, generally scarves. Each tribe has its own style and colour. Their individual combat potential is zero, but they can be irritating in large numbers. You might be able to use them to your advantage. Most important among the tribes are R'al, Juve, Stienn, L'pool and G'ners. Do not on any occasion wear a coloured scarf: Houlgans will only take offence.

Illusory Monsters and Demons

Groms have a liking for this sort of thing. Always remember that the Illus-o-Scope will not be very far away. You WILL be frightened. Gromulan illusions have been known to make a Brontian take fright; note that they can also be on a very large scale.

WEAPONS

Rogue Tracers do not carry many personal arms; the basic weapon is the Catchman, designed by Ulidor Zonie. It shoots out a fine liquid plastic, which takes the form of netting, wraps itself around the prey and thus totally incapacitates him, her or it. Unfortunately it has a high failure rate (33 per cent). Rogue Tracers are skilled in the use of all weapons – blasters, stun guns, even the old-fashioned neutron-swords – but in the last resort they rely on their quick thinking, fast reflexes and superb fitness.

ABILITIES

The mission you are about to undertake will involve your travelling on a strange planet and facing unknown dangers. You must therefore determine your strengths and weaknesses. You will need two dice, a pencil and an eraser. Scores, clues and time factors are to be recorded on the *Adventure Sheet* provided (pages 22–3).

Skill

Roll one die. Add 6 to this number and enter the total in the SKILL box. A high SKILL score shows good fighting ability.

Stamina

Roll two dice. Add 12 to the result and enter the total in the STAMINA box. This shows how fit you are, and how determined you are to succeed in your mission. The higher the score, the longer you will survive. STAMINA will be lost and restored throughout the mission. Always remember to look after yourself: if food is available, have some; if rest is opportune, take it. Remember, you cannot go on for ever like a phozon-powered Crinkletron! A high

STAMINA score will also help you out of difficult situations that require physical effort, such as running, jumping, leaping, swimming, etc.

Luck

Even a top Rogue Tracer needs lots of LUCK to survive. Roll one die. Add 6 to the result and enter the total in the LUCK box. When asked to *Test your Luck*, roll two dice. If the result is *equal to or less than* your current LUCK score, then you have been Lucky. If the result is *greater than* your LUCK score, then you have been Unlucky. Each time you *Test your Luck*, you must reduce your LUCK score by 1 point. There will be times when LUCK points are restored, but if you find that you have no LUCK score, you will be Unlucky in any test.

Fear

Roll one die. Add 6 to the result and enter the total in the FEAR box. Since the Gromulans rely so heavily on illusions calculated to scare, you must at times *Test your Fear Factor*. A bad state of mind can affect your STAMINA and SKILL, and you may be asked to reduce these, if you fail the test. Determine if you are frightened in the same way as you determine LUCK (see above). The FEAR score stays the same throughout the mission.

Time

Time is crucial in this mission. You must complete your task before TIME runs out. You begin with 48 TIME units, which will reduce as you progress in your quest. Note the reductions carefully. Do not waste TIME, but spend TIME gathering clues that will save TIME later on. If your TIME score ever reaches zero, you have failed: the Gromulans have extracted the defence codes from the President's brain.

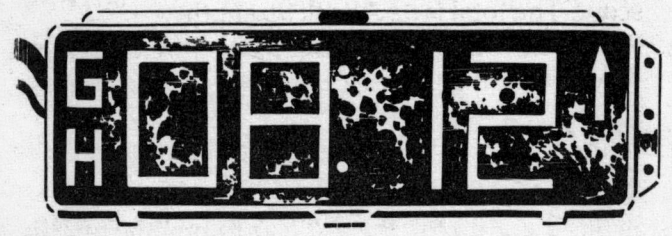

COMBAT

You are armed with a Catchman, which you can use to avoid combat, but you will have to fight your way out of certain situations. If you have to fight, it will usually be hand to hand against one opponent. However, there will be occasions when you have to fight with weapons. In both cases the rules of combat are as follows:

1. Record your opponent's SKILL and STAMINA scores in an Encounter Box on the *Adventure Sheet*.
2. Roll two dice for your opponent. Add its SKILL score. The total is its Attack Strength.
3. Work out your own Attack Strength in the same way, by adding the roll of two dice to your SKILL score.
4. If your Attack Strength is higher than your opponent's, then you have struck a good blow. Subtract 2 points from your opponent's STAMINA score.
5. If your opponent's Attack Strength is greater, then you have been hit. Subtract 2 points from your STAMINA score.
6. If both Attack Strengths are equal, then you have avoided each other's blows.
7. Adjust STAMINA scores and begin the next Attack Round.

8. Repeat the sequence until one STAMINA score reaches zero, when the fight is over.

If you lose, this usually means death, but there will be occasions when you can crawl away and try to build up your STAMINA again.

If you throw double 6 at any time while fighting an Android, then you have found the 'weak spot' and de-activated it.

FEATS AND TASKS

In certain special cases you will be asked to use your STAMINA and SKILL scores for other purposes, such as aerial combat, shooting at craft, etc. In these cases you must enter details in the SPECIAL Encounter Boxes on the *Adventure Sheet*, but you must NOT reduce your real STAMINA score.

Throughout the mission you will be asked to determine distances to jump, leap, swim, etc., by the roll of the dice, and to determine your ability to achieve these feats by adding the roll of a die to your current STAMINA score; you must enter these details in the PHYSICAL TASKS boxes of the *Adventure Sheet*, but you must NOT increase your actual STAMINA score.

GOOD LUCK.

Message ends.

ADVENTURE SHEET

TIME	CLUES	SKILL	STAMINA
48		*Initial Skill =*	*Initial Stamina =*

LUCK
Initial Luck =

FEAR

OXYGEN

CALCULATIONS

Encounter boxes

Skill = Stamina =	Skill = Stamina =	Skill = Stamina =	Skill = Stamina =
Skill = Stamina =	Skill = Stamina =	Skill = Stamina =	Skill = Stamina =
Skill = Stamina =	Skill = Stamina =	Skill = Stamina =	Skill = Stamina =
PHYSICAL TASKS	PHYSICAL TASKS	PHYSICAL TASKS	PHYSICAL TASKS
SPECIAL	SPECIAL	SPECIAL	SPECIAL

1

You have docked into Earth Shuttle Station 23. 'All lines to Ear— Sector 3,' a bright neon light announces. You park your Oberon craft in the short-term airlock and walk down to a dirty-looking ticket-office. There's no one around. You bang on the small plexi-glass window and eventually a MegaCorp Android appears and stutters at you. It should have been out of commission years ago. It has difficulty in understanding your request for a ticket on the next shuttle, but eventually takes your credit card and utters what you will soon recognize as a traditional Earth saying, 'That'll do nicely.' As you trudge away down the corridor, you hear the MegaCorp squeaking at you to 'have a nice day'.

There are about twenty seats in the shuttle, of which only five are occupied. You are directed to your seat and given a copy of the safety procedures by a service Android, and you sit down on something sticky. The Android asks you what you will have. Will you reply:

Nothing?	Turn to 199
A cocktail?	Turn to 69
Food cubes?	Turn to 203

2

You are in an empty chamber. There are exits north-east (turn to 7) and south-west (turn to 395). To the north-west is another tunnel (turn to 27).

3

As you walk along the trench you hear the rumble of machinery below you. You tap the walls on either side and find that they are not solid. You kick hard and the side wall collapses. Inside there is a tunnel with a long conveyor belt full of salt heading back to Roma. You jump on and take a ride. Add 2 STAMINA points and turn to **149**.

4

They sit you down and give you some 'home brew' that tastes like rocket fuel. They obviously think that you too are a fugitive, and they do not question you too closely. They seem to be planning raids on Grom houses in the area and you see that there might be an opportunity of getting to a ComTerm for information. Suddenly a large, bearded rogue with a fat belly comes up to you and punches you in the face. Do you fight back with all your might (turn to **216**) or let him beat you (turn to **141**)?

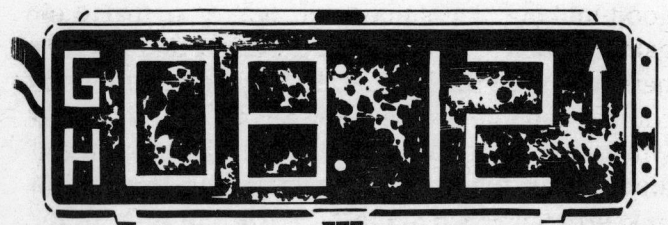

5

You stand at the left terminal. It is obvious that a chess move involving the knight is needed. There is one knight and there are two possible moves. Do you press knight to king's bishop three (turn to 160), or knight to king's rook three (turn to 112)?

6

Suddenly a Grom appears in front of you. This is obviously an Illus-o-Scope image, since he is tall and good-looking. He smiles and tells you that their galactic 'moles' have got information that you are here to rescue the President. All you have to do is confess and you will be richly rewarded. If not, you will never be released and your mission will fail anyway. Do you admit to your mission (turn to 57) or keep silent (turn to 122)?

7

You are in a chamber packed full of food cubes and drink tubes. A Forkliftron is busy stacking small boxes. Do you wish to rest, eat and drink? If you do, deduct 5 TIME units and add 4 STAMINA points. There are exits north-east (turn to **21**) and south-west (turn to **2**).

8

You are correct: A + B − 1 = C. The door slides open and you are faced with an exact replica of yourself, Catchman in hand. You ignore the illusion and it slowly fades away. You see the ComTerm in front of you. You can still hear blasters firing in the distance and you realize that Gus is buying you some precious time. The screen shows:

Pass-code   67   64   73   46   ?

Work out the next number in the series and then turn to that number. If you cannot work it out, turn to **169**.

9

All your senses say no, but you step into the cockpit and the hands grab for your legs. You feel nothing. You sit down where the seat should be and a hand wraps itself around your throat from behind. You slip your hands into the bubbling mud and guess at the location of the rocket starter. The rocket screams and the mud becomes transparent and fades. You look behind you and on the back seat is a piece of Gromulan technology: part of an Illus-o-Scope is wired up to the Zip's shield and was obviously used by the Lurgan to protect his craft. Turn to **211**.

10

You check carefully that there are no Groms or Androids in sight and then stride into the room. The other criminals stare in amazement. The terminal is showing Vidnews as part of high-security Grom TV. Suddenly you see the President with a Grom and two Guards. You look carefully at the coordinates on the left of the screen. The first four groups are standard galactic space codes for Earth Sector North, but you do not recognize the last group. However you take care to memorize the code. You head for the door, but just then a Grom walks in. He emits a muted scream and you move to hit him, but he collapses in a fearful heap. You go through the door and are promptly grabbed by two Excels. Turn to 322.

11

The Android is a domestic-servant type, but is equipped with a sensitive 'people-placer'. It senses you, goes over to a panel and is about to press a button. You rush at it. *Test your Luck*. If you are Lucky, you have caught it before it has hit the button (turn to 236). If you are Unlucky, two Excels appear. They grab you and stun you. You have no chance against them.

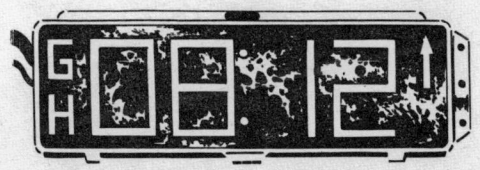

12

Deduct 2 TIME units. You are in a chamber with exits north (turn to **336**) or west (turn to **180**). A southern exit is blocked.

13

You punch Lam in the face and scramble off towards Willi. The manhole it is holding open is rusty. You jump in and Willi follows, dropping the lid and locking it from the inside. You are in a dark, airless hole. There is a passageway ahead and in the distance you can see a faint light. Willi beams up its eyes to give you some light to negotiate the mass of pipes and wires in the tunnel. As you both walk along, Willi trips up and sits in a puddle. You carry on heading for the light; it is coming from a grille up above. Just then you hear a low moan and turn around. Willi has disappeared. The moan is coming from an access shaft down below. Do you decide to climb up to the grille (turn to **192**) or go down the shaft (turn to **255**)?

14

Inside 'Le Spot' it is dark. There are sealed cubicles that take credits. You put one in and a door slides open; you walk in and sit down in the single chair provided. Four set menus appear on a screen. The descriptions are very appetizing. You opt for the most expensive menu, but all you get are the same old cubes in different wrappings. Add 2 STAMINA points and turn to **136**.

15

It stops whining and heads for the street. You let it pass. It dawns on you that in VidEnts there is a certain code about 'showdowns', and it will not be expecting an attack from behind. You pull out the Catchman and fire three spurts. The Excel topples over, but begins to tear the plasti-net apart. You call the men to help and all three of you fall on top of the Android. Its strength is immense. Meanwhile the girl has got into the ZipCar and backed it down towards the fight. You all get out of the way and as the Excel gets up to rip you all to pieces, she blasts the rocket motor at its back. The Android goes down, with plenty of circuitry exposed in its back. Turn to **161**.

16

The others drag the insensible Gigantian away and chain you up. You watch them go out and look for your equipment. Your Chronograph and Catchman are on a chair close by. From what you've heard, you know that you are in Paris and that if you could send out a CodeMatch signal, a 'planted' Android might pick it up. You stretch out your foot, trying to hook the chair and pull it towards you. Roll two dice and add up the total: this is the distance you will have to stretch. Roll one die and add the number to your STAMINA score: this is the limit of your stretch. If the distance is greater than the stretch, you are stuck and you have failed in your mission. If not, turn to **94**.

17

You break open a cube and bite into the sticky brown mess. Just then you hear the roar of Rocket Bikes and, before you can look up, Lopsti bursts in with his gang. You are surrounded. They swing clubs and finger their stun guns. Lopsti wants you to go with them. Do you try to fight (turn to **248**), or will you go with them and try something later (turn to **175**)?

18

You are correct in your calculations: A ÷ C × 2. The door slides open and you walk into a dark room. The only light comes from the glow of a ComTerm. The screen shows a list of options including one called 'Security'. You press this and a sub-menu appears with an option for 'The President'. You smile in admiration at the logical and highly efficient Groms. You press this option but all you get is a sequence of numbers:

1   8   27   ?

Calculate the next number in the sequence and turn to that number. You will be told immediately if you are correct. If you cannot work out the sequence, turn to 124.

19

Kinta Lopsti has beaten you. While he rushes off to call the rest of his gang, you crawl under the stairs of the diner and through a broken air-shaft grille. You hear the gang arrive and Lopsti's tantrum at losing you. They eventually set off with their Rocket Bikes roaring. You crawl out and get back to the diner. It is deserted. You find a Silverhound bus schedule which shows a much-reduced service: the next one leaves in forty-eight gravity hours. The diner operates only when the bus passes through. You are tired and hungry. You find a food dispenser but it will not accept your credit. Will you break it open (turn to 101) or go outside (turn to 230)?

20

The door opens easily and you see a 3-D projection of the galactic rescue fleet. You look around and realize that you are in a Grom transmission studio, which is beaming out the latest news to the Grom ComTerm screens. As you wonder at the size of the rescue fleet, a Grom technician walks in, sees you, shrieks and runs out again. Before you can move, a Gigantian appears, who straightens up as he comes through the door and looks at you. You clutch the neutronsword, but the Gigantian opens its mouth and a Korwellian death bolt shoots out and into your forehead. You have no chance.

21

You are in a chamber with blocked exits to the north and south-east. Do you go:

North-east?	Turn to 62
East?	Turn to 48
South-west?	Turn to 85
West?	Turn to 7

There is also a modern smaller tunnel to the north-west (turn to 82).

22

The Silverhound lurches off and you have to listen to the reps' dirty stories about the pleasure-planet of Luxurus. Eventually you reach Madrid and everybody gets off. Turn to 179.

23

You step into empty space. You spin as though weightless and a beam blasts at you. All that remains of you is some dust in the corner, soon to be swept under the carpet by a faulty Sweepertron.

24

You carry the President through the tunnel and come to the bottom of a spiral staircase. Next to the stairs is a large, very old-fashioned elevator covered in ancient ads that mean nothing to you. You can hear your pursuers. Do you try the elevator (turn to 307) or go up the stairs (turn to 371)?

25

The ladder is strong but very greasy and slippery. There are no features on the smooth steel shafts and you rest for several gravity minutes every once in a while. The light from above gets nearer. Deduct 2 TIME units. Turn to 209.

26

You walk through and the door slides shut. You are in a square glass tank, with water hanging above you! You see no sign of the door you have just used. Suddenly a heavy steel ball with spikes falls out of the water above you and crashes through the floor. Others follow in random positions. Deduct 2 TIME units. *Test your Luck* three times. If you are ever Unlucky, one of the balls has hit you (turn to 201). If you are always Lucky, the balls have weakened the floor. It collapses and you fall through (turn to 333).

27

You speed into the new tunnel and impale yourself on a mass of long steel spikes. The tunnel was merely an illusion, a Grom trick.

28

You lie down flat in the dirty muck. The Rat stops just in front of you. It begins to weld a section of pipe; you keep still. It moves off, but then stops and comes back. A probe emerges from its middle. It will detect your body-heat and blast you. Do you run for it (turn to **289**) or break the probe (turn to **81**)?

29

As you approach the Houlgans, they notice you and slowly surround you. They watch you carefully. Some of them are swinging chains in the air. One of them, who appears to be the leader, asks you if you have any credits. You look at him carefully and see that he has the figure 90 scrawled on his cheek. Do you give them any credits (turn to **147**) or refuse and stand your ground (turn to **287**)?

30

You stand still. The GromPol craft lands and two Excels appear on either side of you. The Android you were following also steps up. They search you thoroughly and find your ID, Catchman and Chronograph. The Android takes your Chronograph. It finds the secret CodeMatch, presses it, and a matching beep is emitted from the Android's arm. Immediately you are in a box: an obvious illusion, but the perspective keeps changing and the walls get larger, smaller, taller and shorter. You are disorientated and wake up in a Grom cell strapped to a Zand Corporation 'Tell Us All'. You embark on a long process of interrogation. You cannot complete your mission.

31

You look around. In the distance two Guard Androids are walking along a wide avenue. It appears as though they are looking for something. You stroll away and turn left down a smaller road, where you notice an old Vidprint shop with some antiquarian floppies in the window. You have not seen floppies since your visit to the Cavod and Xiberti museum when you were a kid. Do you go in (turn to 251) or carry on (turn to 83)?

32

You look around. You are in the grounds of a well-kept house. You walk through the gardens and then hear someone calling: it turns out to be a Grom, who has come out of the house. He tells you that he is glad you have come, since the acidity regulator is faulty, so the Illus-o-Scope will not work and the Androids are incapacitated. He takes you past several immobile Androids to his ComTerm and looks at you expectantly. You cannot resist the opportunity, so you grab him and threaten him into consulting Grom Security with details about the President. The blood drains from his thin face as he quickly fumbles with the keys; then he collapses in a dead faint. Deduct 2 TIME units and turn to **237**.

33

You have calculated correctly: $A + B - 1 = C$. The screen shows a menu and you pick security information. Another menu appears which includes, with typical Grom efficiency, an option for the President. You press this option and all you get is:

$$212 \quad (59) \quad 94$$
$$737 \quad (?) \quad 173$$

If you can supply the correct answer, turn to that section. You will be told that you are correct straight away. If you cannot supply the answer, turn to **194**.

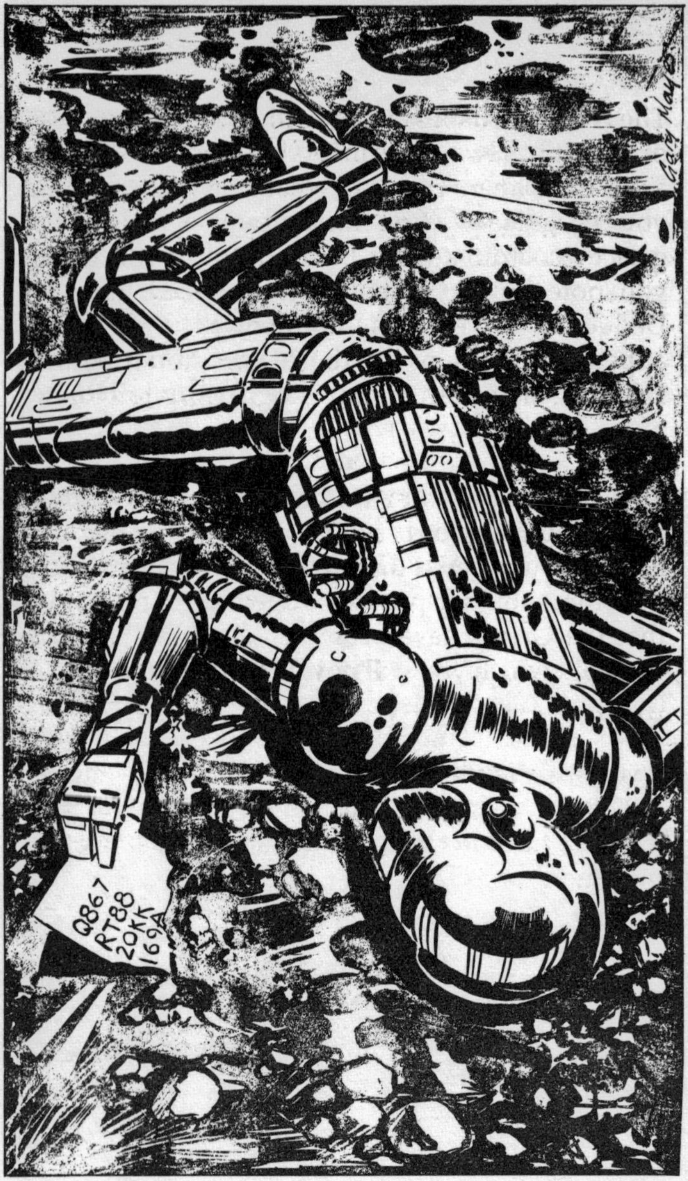
Q867
RT88
20KK
169A

34

The Android rushes out and falls face down in front of you. It has two holes in its side, and in its hand is a piece of paper. You read what's on the paper and you recognize the first three groups of code as the galactic coordinates for London; the fourth group you note down (if you do not already have it). Deduct 2 TIME units. Suddenly a Grom craft appears, its cannons blasting at you. You run for it. Do you go left (turn to **104**) or right (turn to **156**)?

35

You stop in the tunnel when you meet yourself, with neutronsword in hand. You suspect an illusion, but dismiss that thought as the beam slices into the shoulder-pads of your coat. You realize that the Groms have been busy building a replica Android which you will now have to fight.

REPLICA ANDROID   SKILL 9   STAMINA 10

If you win, a small flying leech from Stokex 9 shoots out of the Android's body and fastens itself to your leg. You have to cut it out. Reduce your STAMINA by 2 and turn to **21**.

36

You head off south with Willi towards its master's house. Willi is very chatty: it has been given a Random Personality Chip. Some of its coordination functions have been corrupted, however, and it drops its boxes again. By the time you reach the house you are carrying most of them. There are three Guards at the house, plus an Illus-o-Scope and various other Grom devices. Willi calls you when the coast is clear and points to the door at the top of the stairs. It has not had a chance to get inside and investigate the ComTerm. You run up the stairs and find the door unlocked. Will you rush straight in (turn to **260**), or do you prefer to check out a possible alarm circuit (turn to **301**)?

37

You are in a chamber with blocked exits south, north-east and north-west. There is an unmarked door (turn to **20**), and exits west (turn to **353**) and east (turn to **116**).

38

You press 'A' and on the screen you see:

Q867   RT88   20KK

You recognize this as the open code for London base. Then the screen goes blank. Turn to **368**.

39

The shuttle lands in the dark segment of the planet, in what appears to be a desolate area of Sector 3. There are no habitation lights and you assume that this base station was built in the days when shuttles needed huge landing-areas. All the passengers troop out into the station. You look up and see the familiar Rocket-a-Hire sign and go over to a shoddy counter. There is no Android on duty. You stand there reading ZipCar brochures while all the other passengers file towards the Silverhound which is waiting outside, smoke belching from its rocket outlets: its destination is Madrid. In the far corner a Sweepertron takes a break from its work and looks at you. Do you wait around for a ZipCar (turn to **145**), talk to the Android (turn to **357**), or join the others in the Silverhound (turn to **373**)?

40

You wake up and find yourself lying by an anti-gravity swimming-pool. As you stare at the block of water, the Grom comes out and apologizes for the deceit, 'but it does make the game more interesting when the stakes seem to be life itself'. He gives you food and drink (add 4 STAMINA points), then talks to you for several gravity hours and lets slip that he is highly placed in Gromulan HQ. In the corner near the house is a ComTerm which occasionally beeps. When the Grom leaves for a moment, you catch a glimpse of the Galactic President on the screen. Do you approach the ComTerm (turn to **242**), or stay where you are (turn to **190**)?

41

The ZipCar performs well and logs in a flight path for Madrid. You set it for 'autoland' and key in the required landing-request data. You relax as the craft does all the work for you and sets you down with a gentle bump. Deduct 2 TIME units.

You get out and snap the plexi-glass top down. You notice that the Illus-o-Scope is beginning to work again; it is filling the cockpit with blood. As you walk away you look back and see a GromPol looking over the ZipCar; you suddenly realize that it is stolen. You will not be able to return to it. Turn to 179.

42

You run very fast, but two Androids appear behind you and give chase. Roll three dice and add up the total: this is the speed of the Androids. If it is greater than your STAMINA, they have made you change direction (turn to 262). If your STAMINA is equal to or greater than their speed, you have outrun them. You carry on for a while and then stop by a large building and look around (turn to 59).

43

The Android tells you it is from the GUS series (Genus Undercover and Subterfuge) and sets a fast pace to the east. It weaves through the side-streets and soon you are both standing outside a Grom mansion. Gus does not hesitate on seeing the two Guards at the door. It tells you to wait and then approaches the Guards, walking backwards and dragging one foot. The Guards walk towards Gus, curiosity circuits buzzing. As they draw level, Gus takes the first guard's head off with a hand blow and kicks a chunk out of the second's middle. You rush to help, while the Guards kick, gurgle and buzz. You sit on one until it self-destructs. Then you follow Gus into the house. 'ComTerm should be on the floor above,' it tells you as it adopts a position by the elevator, blaster in one hand, stun gun in the other. When you reach the top you can hear the swish of blaster fire. You realize that you haven't much time. There is a door ahead: turn to **92**.

44

You are in a chamber which has obviously been refurbished in hi-tech Grom style. There is a Vidscreen on the wall with an image of you and a warning that you are probably in the Inner London base. Deduct 2 TIME units. There is a door marked 'Strictly no unauthorized entry' (turn to **334**), and exits west (turn to **71**) or east (turn to **131**).

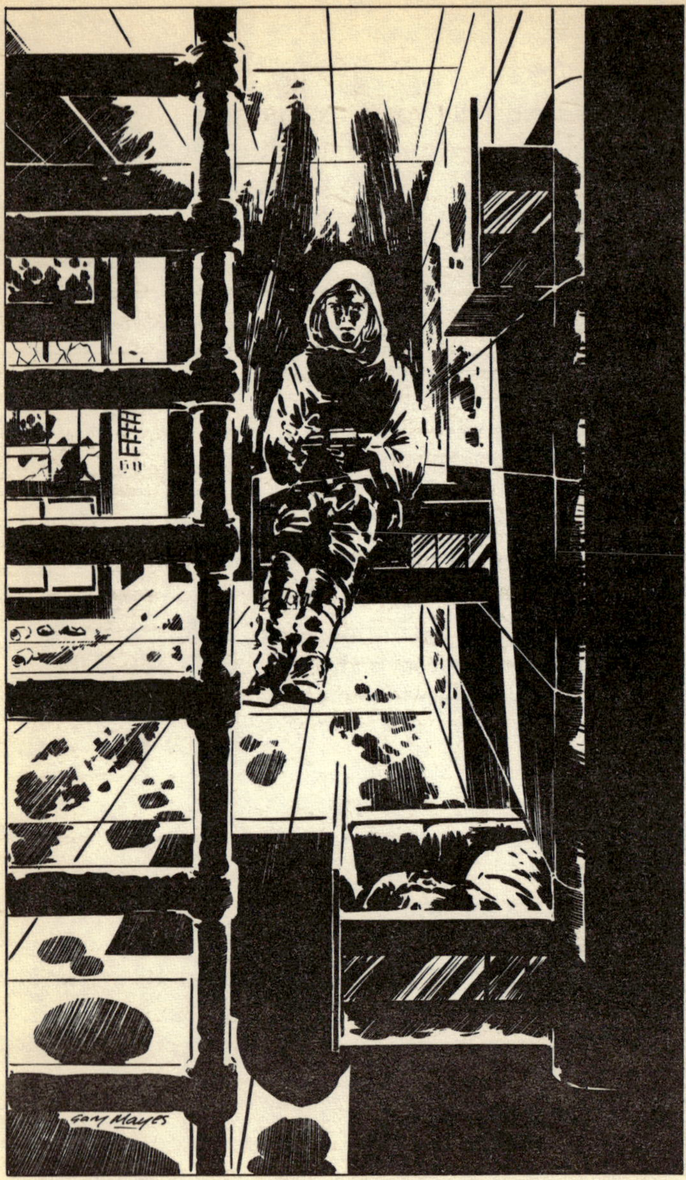
Gary Mayes

45

You are very tired by the time you land at Roma terminal. You check when the bus is due to leave and set an alarm on your Chronograph. You stagger out of the terminal and the first sign you see is that of a Fast Food and Sleep Unit. It looks very shabby and some dubious characters from the bus are heading for it.

'That'll do nicely,' squeals the gate mechanism when you slip your credit in. Inside you pick up some cubes advertised as Virwat-duck flavour and sit on a broken chair munching the tasteless mush. You look around you: rubbish litters the area and is being kicked about by all sorts of rogues; a couple you recognize are worth a few hundred credits, but you are far too tired. Sitting on one of the sleep units is a woman cleaning a stun gun. She looks familiar and stares at you. Then she lies down and closes up her unit. You do the same. Add 6 STAMINA points.

When you get up, she is just leaving. Do you follow her (turn to 153) or hurry on in your search (turn to 142)?

46

Deduct 2 TIME units. The one straight ahead gives you the best chance of using the Catchman. You fire: throw a die. If you throw 1–3, it has failed (turn to 207). If you throw 4–6, you have caught one of the gang (turn to 345).

47

Suddenly the scene changes. You are standing by a beautiful beach, the sun is setting and you know that you are rich and powerful, but you cannot remember any details. You are about to remember, when your Rogue Tracer mind-training reasserts itself and you know that this is just another Grom brain-game. The scene fades into darkness. Four doors appear. A voice tells you that three of them lead to death and one leads to freedom, and that the choice is yours. You are also forced into a decision by the wall behind you glowing red hot and pushing you towards the doors. The doors are marked with chess symbols. Do you choose:

The pawn?	Turn to 23
The knight?	Turn to 166
The rook?	Turn to 212
The bishop?	Turn to 225

48

You are in a chamber with a blocked exit south-east and exits east (turn to 331), west (turn to 21) and north-west (turn to 62).

49

You head towards the right-hand shelter. The bull is ready to charge. You wait for it to get close enough to prod with the spear.

BULL   SKILL 7   STAMINA 12

If you reduce the bull's STAMINA to 6, you have struck its shoulder circuits. There are some sparks and smoke, and you run into the shelter. You look around, but there is no door: you must try the other shelter. Turn to 378.

50
You keep your hands away from your coat and walk towards the Android. You hear one of the men say, 'He is mad, his circuits are all twisted.' The Android whips out its gun, but then stands stock-still making a whirring noise. Deduct 2 TIME units. Do you try to immobilize it (turn to 205) or to get more information from the people in the bar (turn to 306)?

51
You are in Red room, Level 1. There are two doors leading downwards. Reduce OXYGEN level by 1. Do you go left (turn to 97) or right (turn to 181)?

52
A shot blasts near you and you collapse. The Androids approach you, while the craft is blasted out of the sky by Grom defence missiles. They grab you just as you begin to black out. Turn to 322.

53
Test your Luck. If you are Lucky, turn to 395. If you are Unlucky, turn to 67.

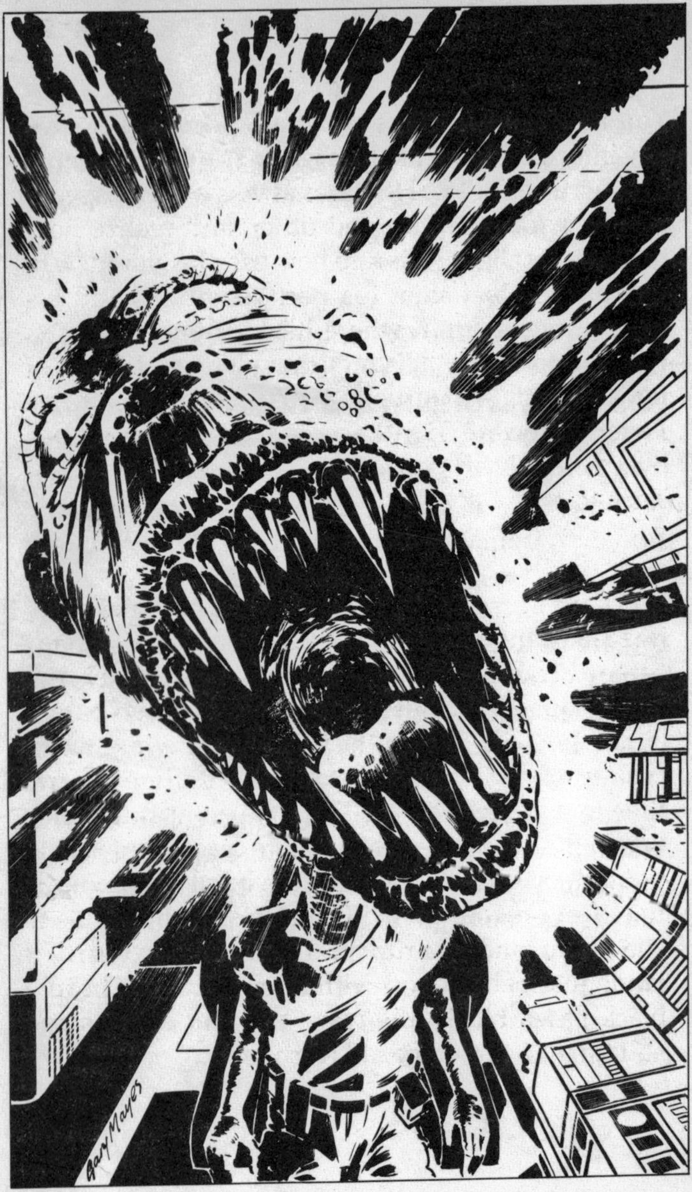
Gary Mayes

54

You are right to refuse. Rogue Tracers never give any information on likely targets. The Grom accepts this fact and smiles. He stares at you without speaking. You look him up and down and realize how remarkably slight he is and how easy he would be to overpower. Just then his neck lengthens and his head stretches from where he is sitting to right in front of your face. His mouth widens and is full of fangs about to bite your head off! *Test your Fear Factor*. If you are frightened, reduce your STAMINA by 1 point. Then you are allowed back on the bus. Turn to **219**.

55

You have broken a beam. Everything becomes fluid; images change. You find yourself on a large black square. You look around and see similar black and white squares and giant chess pieces all laid out on either side of you. To the left a giant white pawn rushes towards you and stops in the white square, then to your right a black knight leaps out and lands with a thump on the black square diagonally next to yours. You know it's an illusion, but it has a powerful effect on your brain. The black knight begins to chase you, and you run for the edge of the board. It lands just behind you with a loud crash. Ahead a black pawn blocks the way. You can either stand still (turn to **129**) or go left (turn to **172**).

56

You are in a chamber with exits east (turn to **395**) and north (turn to **288**).

57

The Grom smiles and looks you up and down. Then all your molecules are blasted apart.

58

You walk up to it. Do you demand a 'showdown' in the street (turn to **15**) or ask it where its horse is (turn to **214**)?

59

Across from the building you see a flashing sign: '–INOS C–UB'. You walk up to the front door, which is just a bead curtain. You walk through and see a juke projecting an old Galaxy Ents Promo. You walk up to the dispenser and press for a Mangola tube. You look around. There are many 'untraced' rogues about – rich pickings if you were in the mood. In the far corner a fight begins. Someone gets punched and falls into the projection. He is followed by Orvium, who stands over him and kicks him. Turn to **275**.

60

You sneak past the house. You are tempted by the launch, but if it is a Grom craft it will be well guarded. Just then you see an Excel Android two hundred metres ahead. It is right in your path and looking straight towards you. Do you jump into the bushes (turn to **164**) or stay exactly where you are (turn to **206**)?

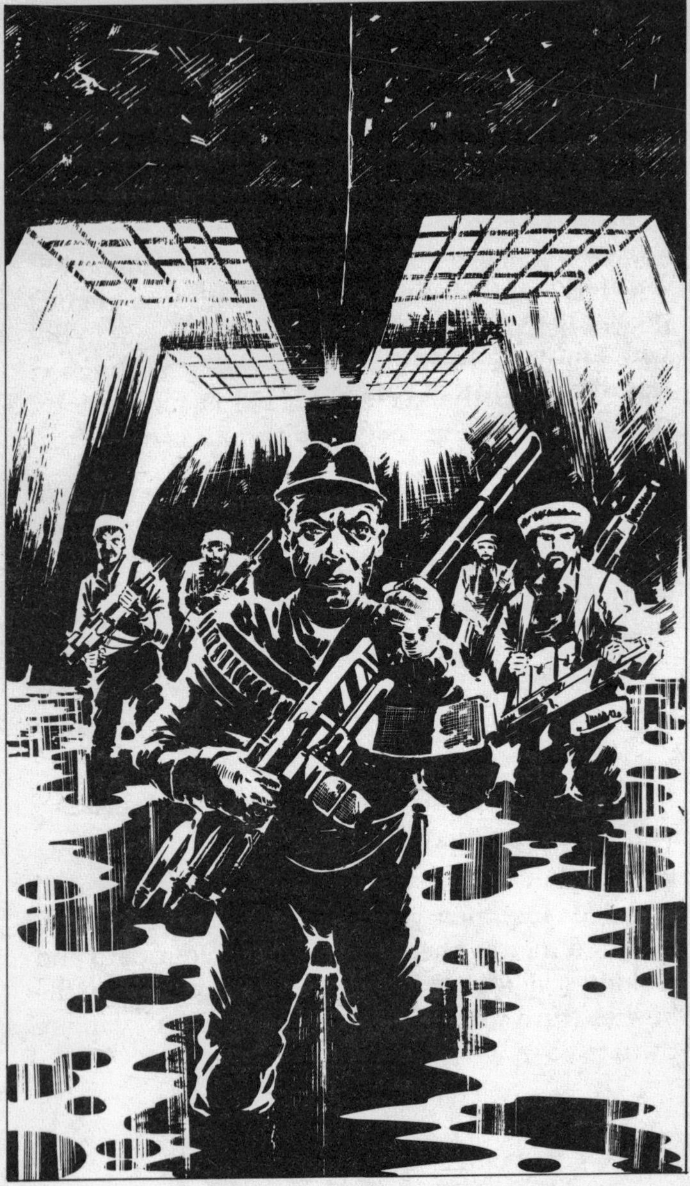

61

The woman lies in the water. You get up and turn around as you hear a noise. You are faced with five men, all heavily armed. One of them calls out, 'Felina!' The woman mutters, 'Kill the intruder.' You wisely decide to run for it, and they chase you. Throw three dice and add up the result. If this is greater than your STAMINA score, they have caught you, and you have no chance against them. If it is less than or equal to your STAMINA score, you have outdistanced them. Turn to 376.

62

You are in a chamber full of crates. There are exits blocked by rubble to the north and west. Deduct 2 TIME units. Which way do you go:

East?	Turn to 139
North-east?	Turn to 318
South-west?	Turn to 21
South?	Turn to 48

There is also a smaller modern tunnel heading south-east (turn to 82).

63

The Android is disguised as an administrative support. It is a good idea to attack it, for you know its circuits very well. You throw your weight on its back and as it falls into the bushes, you gently press the back of its left ear. Automatic functions cease. You reach inside its mouth and rip out the Com board to stop it transmitting distress signals. You have thirty gravity seconds before self-destruct sets in. You can ask one question:

Where is the President kept?	Turn to 259
Where are Grom secret records kept?	Turn to 339
How can I get into the administrative building?	Turn to 281
What do the Groms know about my mission?	Turn to 102

64

You are correct: 1 cubed, 2 cubed, 3 cubed, etc. The terminal requests your question. You key in, 'Is the President in Madrid?' It answers in the negative. 'Where is the President?' It replies, 'He is kept at a high-security Base, reference 169A . . .' The message stops, the screen goes blank, and then you are asked for your family code letter. You press random keys, but it begins to flash 'ILLEGAL ACCESS'. You memorize the little information you got out of it. Turn to 124.

65

You take a risk! You press the starter and pump at the pedal. *Test your Luck*. If you are Unlucky, the bike does not start immediately and Lopsti has had time to hit you with a stun shot (turn to 95). If you are Lucky, the bike starts and you are in the air (turn to 184).

66

You walk along the street. Here the area is overgrown, trees poke out of windows, buildings are crumbling and grass grows on the roads. Suddenly you hear a growl and in front of you stands a huge white wolf. You pull out your Catchman and fire. *Test your Luck*. If you are Lucky, turn to 303; if you are Unlucky, turn to 355.

67

A strange dark creature blocks the tunnel. Its arms end in sharp pointed teeth that move in and out. It has no head, but there is a large eye in the centre of its body. If you do not wish to fight, turn to 85.

LEECH   SKILL 7   STAMINA 8

If you win, turn to 395.

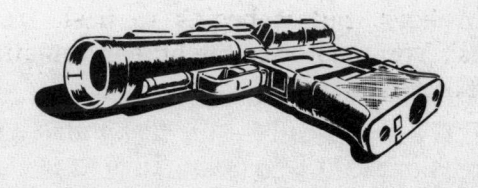

68

You suggest a game to be played on her parents' ComTerm. She tells you that she is not allowed in there. You tell her it's a code-breaking game. She stands there debating it in her mind. Her image grows until she appears to be three metres tall. She then assumes her real height; small silver stars circle her head, and she agrees. She touches a panel in what seems to be a blank wall and a section of the floor moves and carries both of you through the ceiling. You notice a communicator on her wrist and you realize that she could summon Excel guards if she wanted. She takes you to a door and tells you that it's in there. You ask her to go and get a Vidcorder and laserpen for the game. You stress that you want the real thing, no illusions. She skips off, calling for Beany the Butler. Deduct 2 TIME units. By the side of the door you see a panel with the following sequence:

54	(12)	9
18	(?)	2

Work out the correct missing number and go to that section. You will be told at once that you are correct. If you cannot work out the missing number, turn to **124**.

69

A drink will only cloud your judgement and you will need a clear head for the task in front of you. Reduce your SKILL by 1 point. Turn to **39**.

70

You leave the grounds of the house with Willi just as a ring of fire appears all round the building. Willi tells you that the Illus-o-Scope has been re-activated and suggests a very rapid exit out of the area. As you walk along a deserted street you ask Willi about the central administrative building. It tells you that the Plaza de Toros is exclusively for Androids and is built underground below the bullring, a part of the Grom Ents Complex. Willi knows that there is a way into the building through the Ents Complex. As Willi talks, it disguises itself as a GromPol guard, but you have to keep stopping to pick up the bits that it continually drops. Turn to **200**.

71

You are in a chamber which, by its smell, seems to be the Grom rubbish dump. There are lots of snail shells around, many with decomposing snails inside. Now and again you catch sight of a large rat delving into the rubbish. There are exits east (turn to **44**) and south (turn to **332**).

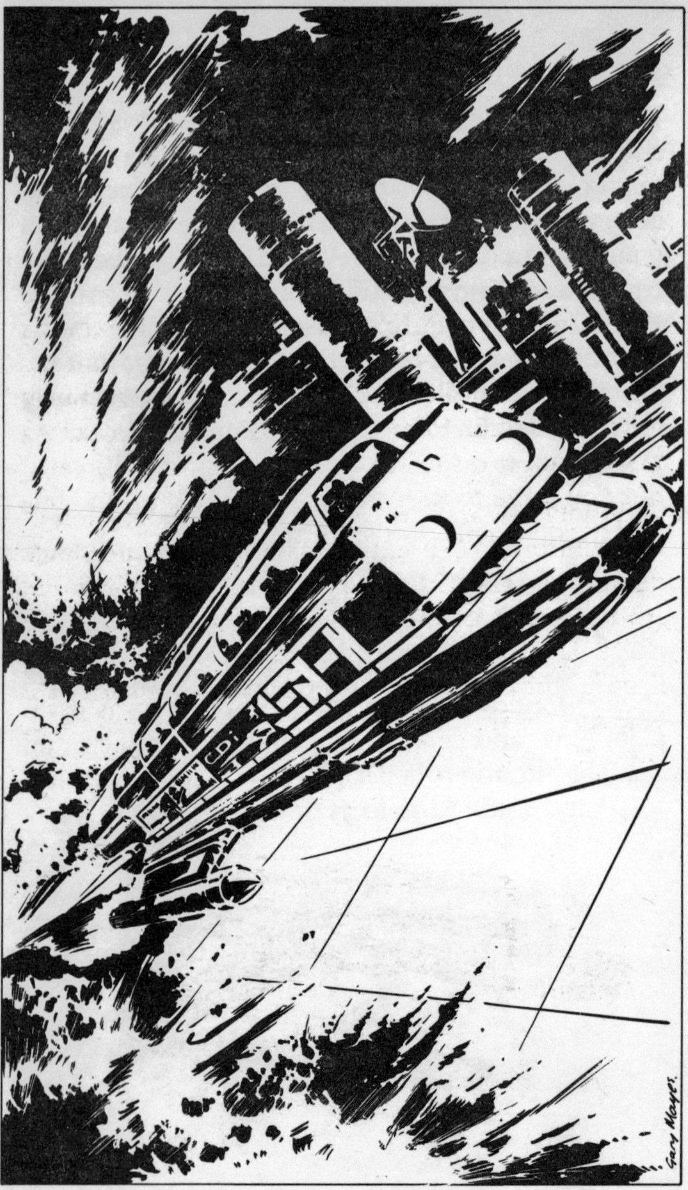
Gary Mayes.

You board the bus. All the passengers are from the shuttle. You sit down and strap up; the Silverhound lurches and then speeds off. From their conversation, you detect that most of the passengers are sales reps; the main topic is the price of salt-mining equipment. One passenger, obviously a Grom, sits ahead in the small first-class section. He is being attended by his own Android. You begin to doze off, while the Vidscreen in front of you shows endless adverts from Galactic Ents Inc. Deduct 2 TIME units.

Suddenly you wake up with a start. You look out of the window to see lights flashing. The bus slows down and lands in a swirl of dust. Two GromPol Androids get in and announce that they want to check IDs. When they see your Rogue Tracer's licence, they grab you and throw you outside. Do you run for it (turn to 385) or go along with them (turn to 119)?

73

You race down the tunnel, splashing through the sludge and water. You see the occasional dark shape and then you see more and more. You stop when you realize that they are giant rats with huge fangs. You are quickly surrounded by about two dozen of them. You pull out your Catchman and fire at the nearest bunch. *Test your Luck* three times. Each time you are Unlucky, deduct 3 STAMINA points for the bites you receive.

You crawl out of the sewer on a rusty ladder and you see a commercial transport in front of you marked with the name 'Escargot' and a circle with a horizontal line through it. It seems to be about to take off. Do you stow away on the transport (turn to **239**) or return to the Silverhound terminal (turn to **134**)?

74

You cannot restrain yourself. Jose and the gang watch in wonder as you flip over and take on the rogue in unarmed combat.

ROGUE   SKILL 8   STAMINA 8

If you win, you wrap up the rogue in plasti-net, 'mark' him and give the gang share discs in the 'kill', which should keep them from going hungry for many months. Add 1 LUCK point. You go through the manhole. Turn to **114**.

75

You reach the Silverhound terminal and rush forward to slip in your credit. But there is no need to hurry: there are only two other passengers, both Androids. They stand still and buzz to each other. You get on the bus, find a comfortable place and watch a TravelVid about Roma. Apparently the Gromulans believe that there is some connection between the founding of Roma and their race. You eat several cubes and then go to sleep. Add 3 STAMINA points. Deduct 2 TIME units and turn to **157**.

76

When you approach Paris you are automatically logged into a Galactic Ents commentary on the city. It looks beautiful, with its heavily overgrown buildings. You fly over an old expressway which is solid with rusted vintage cars – apparently the scene of the greatest traffic jam the planet ever had in the previous century when Earth was still heavily populated. You land the Silverhound at Paris terminal. When you get out of the craft, you are promptly arrested by two GromPol Androids for unauthorized flying. Do you fight your way out (turn to **399**), or do you go quietly (turn to **168**)?

77

You take off for cover, weaving, twisting and flipping over, using all your Rogue Tracer agility, but even so a stun shot hits you in the back. It is a mild blast, but it stops you in your tracks. You go inside the hotel. Reduce your STAMINA by 1 point and turn to **197**.

78

When you reach Paris you see a beautiful overgrown city. A Galactic Ents commentary automatically starts up on your ZipCar speakers and while the vehicle follows the pre-set landing coordinates, you look out and play the tourist. The commentary is interrupted by a Mangola advert and then the craft autolands. When you get out of the ZipCar, two GromPol Androids appear and arrest you for flying without paying the toll charges. Deduct 2 TIME units. Turn to **314**.

79

You follow the main street aimlessly. You stop and look around you. Turn to **117**.

80

You arrive at the Silverhound terminal with little time to spare. There are many people milling around. A sign flashes above the boarding-gate: 'BUS FULL'. You rush towards the Android standing by the door. You show it your Rogue Tracer's ID; there is a sharp intake of air into its system, it boards the bus and throws off a rather elderly woman. She is very cross and the other passengers stare at you while you take your seat. You sit next to an Excel and try to get some rest, but you find it difficult because there is a large group of natives at the front who keep chattering and screaming at one another while they pass around drink tubes and food cubes. They do not offer you any. Deduct 2 TIME units. Turn to 45.

81

You snap off the probe and it immediately begins to blast in all directions. Roll two dice. If you throw a double, it has hit you with a deadly blast. Otherwise it retires back to where it came from and you carry on towards the light. You come to a vertical shaft. Turn to **192**.

82

You speed along the tunnel and eventually reach a chamber with cells leading off it. In the far cell you can see an Android lying on the floor in the early stages of self-destruct. You rush over and there in front of you is the President; his clothing is tattered, he has a space dagger in his hand and he is breathing very heavily. You try to calm him down. Just then you hear a noise and turn around. The President Android stabs you in the back.

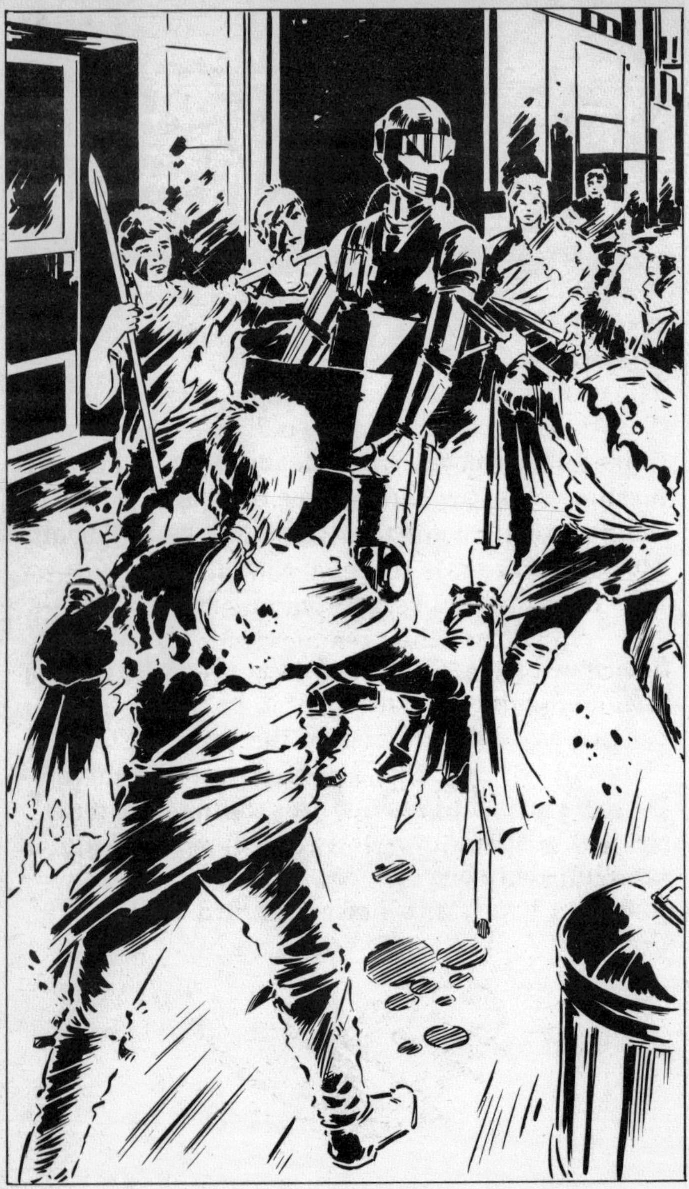

83

You can see a large circular building in the distance, but as you head towards it you feel the throb of your Chronograph, which is now pre-set to CodeMatch with 'planted' Androids. You look around you. To your left is an Android with some boxes in its hands. It is being intimidated by a bunch of Houlgans. Do you help the Android (turn to **276**), or do you prefer to keep a low profile (turn to **319**)?

84

Three of the gang crumple up, entangled in the plasti-net. You run for the nearest Rocket Bike, jump on, start up and take off. You turn around and notice that no one is pursuing you. Just then the fuel tank explodes and as you plummet to your death you remember the remote-destruct anti-theft device, which is 'widely available in all good stores throughout the galaxy'.

85

Deduct 2 TIME units. You are in a chamber with a blocked exit south, and exits west (turn to **53**) or north (turn to **267**).

86

'So am I, in a manner of speaking,' he says as he continues to fly behind the bus and is joined by three other heavily armed ZipCars. It is obvious that they intend to attack the Silverhound over the mountains. You peer over his shoulder and notice a scan monitor showing up the Catchman in your coat. Your section of the cockpit is suddenly sealed and you hear the sound of gas. Turn to **386**.

87

You walk along what seems to be an old sewage system, wading through water and sludge. You come to a fork in the tunnel. Do you take the left-hand branch (turn to **372**) or the right (turn to **202**)?

88

You open the small door and find yourself in a long, empty corridor. You tread gently and watch out for alarm beams. Eventually you see a door marked EXIT, and another door marked:

> GromPol and Excel series only. Strictly no admittance to any other Androids.

Which door do you take, the EXIT (turn to **194**) or the other one (turn to **383**)?

89

Bracing yourself against the force, you press the Thruster. The acceleration flattens you into the seat as you speed up to ten times the normal maximum. The Grom is left far behind. You cannot hope to steer, but have to rely on auto-pilot. As you climb to maximum height, the fuel runs out and the rockets shut off, but you have time to glide in one of three directions. Which one do you choose:

Left?	Turn to 178
Right?	Turn to 234
Straight on?	Turn to 398

90

As you walk along, you stumble over a block of stone. Noticing some writing carved on it, you brush away the grass to reveal the legend 'Madrid 180 km', with an arrow pointing in the direction you have just come from. You set off back along the road. Deduct 4 TIME units and turn to 327.

91

You settle back in your seat. The door slides open and the Grom comes in with two GromPols. He throws you a food cube and asks if you want a wash. When you have freshened up, you speed off to catch the Silverhound. Add 2 STAMINA points. Deduct 2 TIME units and turn to 381.

92

You stand by the door and see the following on a panel:

$$\begin{array}{ccc} 6 & 9 & 14 \\ 8 & 13 & 20 \\ 4 & 5 & ? \end{array}$$

There is a numeric keyboard for keying in the correct number in the sequence. Groms are logical people of great intellect. If you find the missing number, go to that section and you will be told straight away that you are correct. If you cannot work out the missing number, turn to **169**.

93

The door slides open. You jump left and fire your Catchman at the rogue on the left. The plasti-net envelops him. The second pulls out a blaster, but you are on him before he can fire.

ROGUE   SKILL 7   STAMINA 8

If you lose, you are put into a sack and thrown into the River Tiber. If you win, turn to **138**.

94

You pull the chair towards you with your feet until you can reach the Chronograph. There are two possible settings: one sends a beam a short distance but in all directions (turn to **130**), the other sends a long thin beam in one direction (turn to **187**).

95

The gang tie you up and secure you to a Rocket Bike. They take off and drop you into some remote scrubland. Your mission is over.

96

You swim into the river, find a way out and climb up, soaking wet. Add 2 LUCK points. Looking around, you find that the Silverhound terminal is directly opposite. You check with your Chronograph and rush towards it just in time to see the bus take off. You have missed it! You look desperately around for a craft, but there is only one ZipCar in the craft-park, and it has someone sitting inside. Do you approach the ZipCar owner (turn to **154**), or go back into the city to look for transport (turn to **243**)?

97

You are in Yellow room, Level 2. Reduce OXYGEN by 1. There is one door up (turn to **51**), a left door down (turn to **196**) and a right door down (turn to **146**).

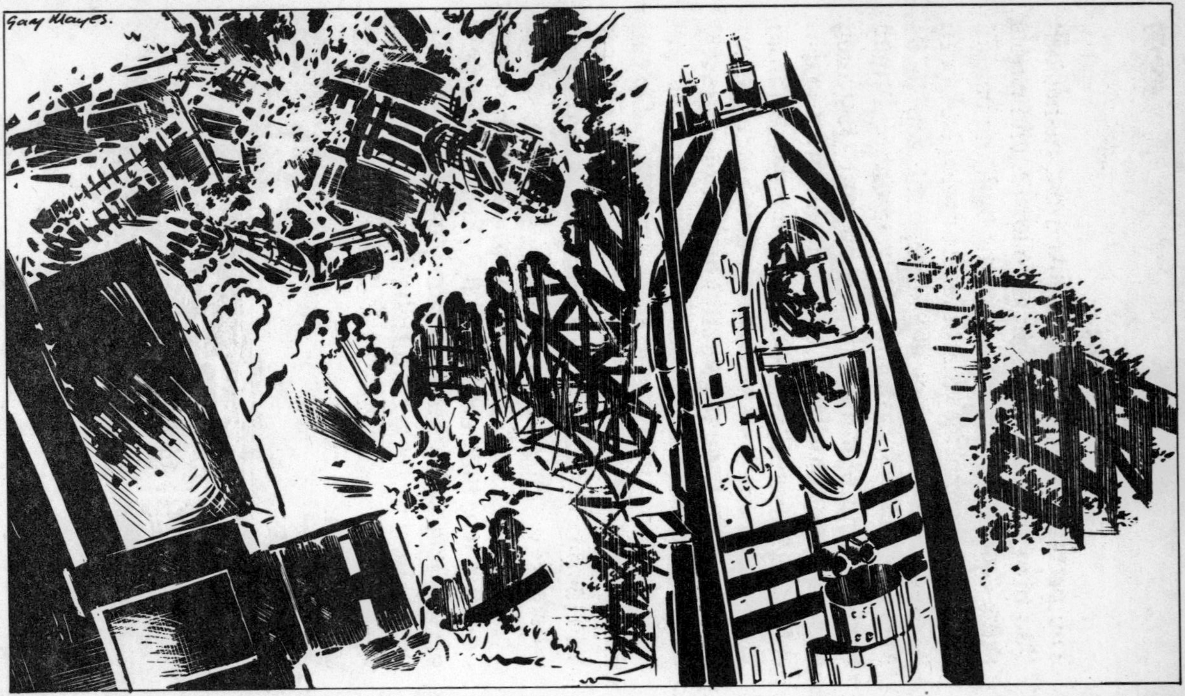
Gary Mayes.

98

You pretend to go in, and the Android rushes off. You turn around and begin to follow it, and notice three GromPols coming out of the building behind you. This confirms that the Android has been 'turned' and now has a Vidgraph of you in its memory. You must destroy it! It heads for a rusty metal structure of no apparent purpose. Just then you hear explosions and see a ZipCar with Houlgan colours flash past. It fires its cannons at the Android and you. The first shot hits the Android, the second . . . *Test your Luck*. If you are Lucky, turn to **195**. If you are Unlucky, turn to **52**.

99

You approach the two Androids and ask them where you can get transport to the nearest city. They inform you that only shuttle links are running now and that the next shuttle is due in seventy-two gravity hours. They leave you and speed off in their craft. Deduct 2 TIME units. Will you wait for the next Silverhound (turn to **188**), or set off on foot (turn to **283**)?

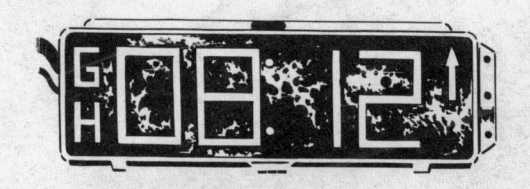

100

You can see no way of making the door slide open, and then you realize that it must be pushed. It is heavy and made of wood. You slip inside and find that you are in a hallway with three doors leading off it. While you debate which one to go through, the middle door opens and out comes an Android carrying a jar. Do you take cover (turn to **11**) or attack the Android (turn to **236**)?

101

It's a risk worth taking. You kick it open and chew some cubes. There is no alarm and you can eat your fill. Add 2 STAMINA points and deduct 2 TIME units. You then go outside. Turn to **291**.

102

While the decay begins at its feet, the Android replies, 'Groms know of rescue attempt, they also know of "planted" Androids. They do not know who else is involved. They are monitoring the rescue fleet . . . You . . .' The decay eats into all its speech functions and as you get up the Android disappears, leaving a pungent odour. Deduct 2 TIME units and turn to **31**.

103

After walking for many gravity hours in the thick forest, you arrive at a fork in the road. Do you turn left (turn to **268**) or right (turn to **90**)?

104

You dodge to the left, straight into the path of a cannon shot. You take no more interest in this mission.

105

You stand there as the door opens. They come in and stand side by side fingering their stun guns. Willi suddenly leaps out with amazing speed and attacks the one on the right. You kick the stun gun out of the other's hand and engage it in unarmed combat.

GUARD ANDROID   SKILL 9   STAMINA 10

If you win, Willi has disabled the other Guard. Turn to **70**.

106

You try to move off to search the house. She puts you into a snake-pit: snakes are underfoot, on top of you and winding around your arms and legs. You try to remember that this is an illusion. *Test your Fear Factor*. If you are frightened, reduce your STAMINA by 1. You scream that you'll play with her. Turn to **68**.

107

The three gang members are tough street-fighters and you are shattered. Lopsti realizes that the diner's craft-park is not a safe place to hang around. He kicks one of his gang and tells him to put you on to the back of a Rocket Bike. You get on and wait for another member of the gang to smash a food-cube dispenser and steal the contents, before you all roar off in a stink of rocket fuel. Turn to **354**.

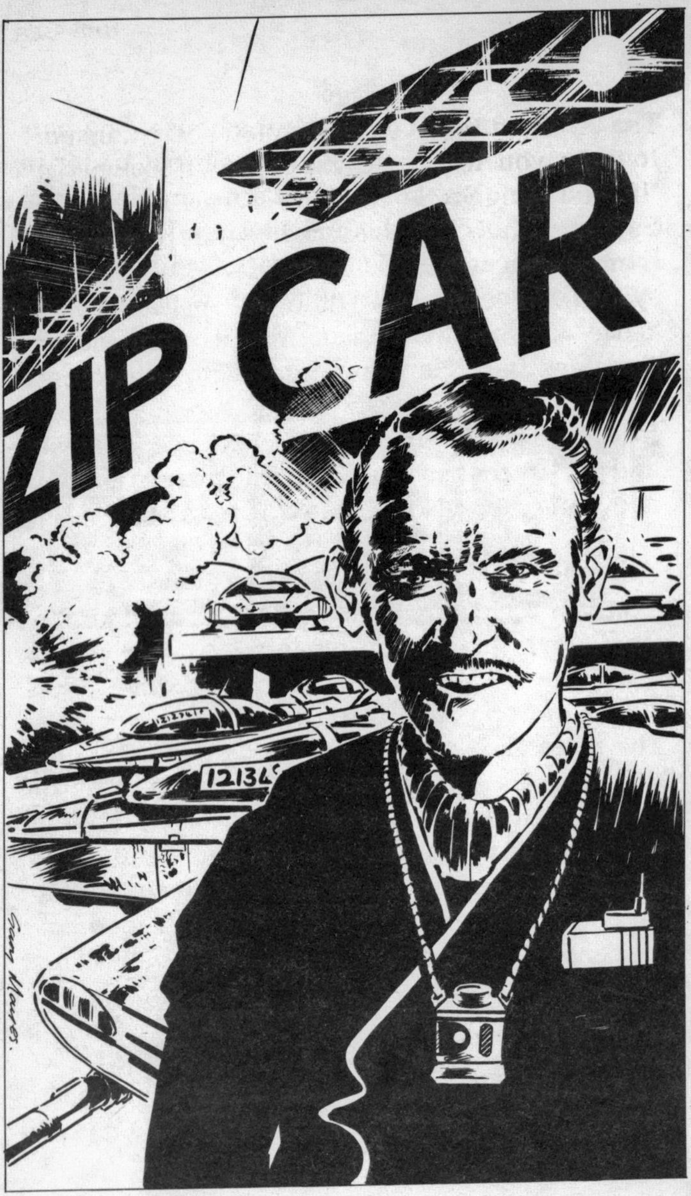
ZIP CAR

108

The Android tells you that you'll need transport. It takes you to a used ZipCar centre owned by 'Honest' Luig Six. Most of the cars are rusty heaps, but Luig Six is not prepared to part with any of them. He shows you a Grom Vidlaw forbidding the sale of any transports without a special Grom licence. The Android takes him to one side and threatens him. He comes back with a frightened smile on his face and is willing to accept a fair price for a serviceable ZipCar. You check the fuel levels and get directions from the Android. You speed above the city, heading north. Turn to **224**.

109

You walk up to what seems to be the front door. You find it open and as you step into the house you call out. There is no answer. There are three doors. Which one do you go through:

Left?	Turn to **26**
Right?	Turn to **120**
Centre?	Turn to **361**

110

After a while a small Gromulan with an Excel on either side of him appears and walks along the row. He stops in front of you and holds up a strange device. It projects a beam and tries to brainscan you. As a Rogue Tracer you are protected against this. 'So, we have a Tracer here,' he squeaks. The Excels grab you, take you to a room and leave you there. In the corner is a ComTerm showing pictures of the President. Do you want to approach the ComTerm (turn to **316**) or stay where you are (turn to **296**)?

111

You reach the shelter just as the bull slams its horns into the heavy plastic. You look around the shelter: there are two short spears there, which seem to be armed with impact neuronsplat. You guess that there must be a proper entrance behind one of the three shelters. You will have to cross to the others to find out. You pick up the spears and rush out. Which shelter do you pick, the left one (turn to **378**) or the right one (turn to **49**)?

112

The door slides open and you walk into a darkened room. The door slides shut behind you. You are in a Grom Moebius Time-Trap. Time will have no meaning for you; gravity seconds will seem to take years to pass. You are doomed and your mission is over.

113

You weave up and down and turn to fight off the Grom. The cannons do not respond: there is no phozon auto-shot as on your Oberon craft. Two final shots slam into you and the Mark III dives out of control. You are already dead.

114

You are in a tunnel. It is dark and damp. There are many pipes of various sizes stretching into the distance. Deduct 2 TIME units. As you walk towards a faint light, you hear a rattle behind you. You turn around and see two red eyes slowly coming towards you. They belong to a 'Service Rat', which is inspecting the sub-ducts and making repairs. You know that these machines are equipped with blasters to remove any debris or blockages. Do you decide to let it pass over you (turn to 28), or would you rather run towards the end of the tunnel (turn to 289)?

115

You get up and try to clear your head while you slip on the gloves.

GIGANTIAN   SKILL 10   STAMINA 12

If you win, turn to **16**.

116

Test your Luck. If you are Lucky, turn to **336**. If you are Unlucky, turn to **374**.

117

You notice two Guards approaching, so you turn a corner and head west. You walk along a wide avenue. At one crossroads there is a small market. Groups of people stand around, some natives and several Felines from Wistas 4. Tucked into a corner basement you see a flashing sign: 'SLEEP/EAT'. An arrow points down. You know that you will soon need some rest. Do you want to enter the basement (turn to **228**) or carry on with your quest (turn to **324**)?

118

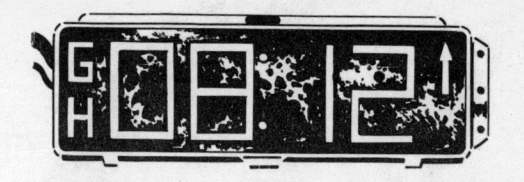

On the way to London, you begin to cross a short stretch of sea. Suddenly a laser blast hits your craft and everything, including you, is burned to a cinder.

119

You are pushed into the GromPol craft and made to stand in front of the Grom commander, who is sitting down. He watches you very carefully, then asks who you are tracing. Do you give him a name (turn to **312**) or refuse to speak (turn to **54**)?

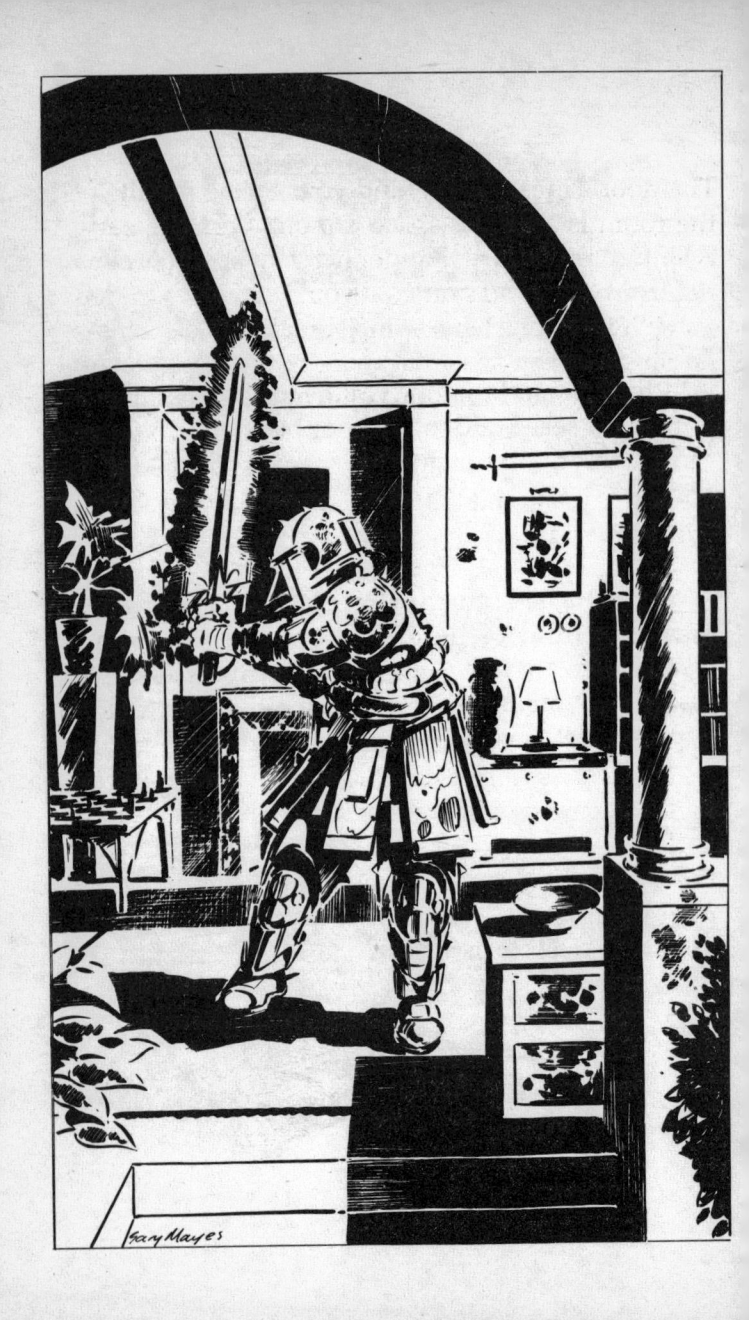
Gary Mayes

120

The door slides shut behind you. In the middle of the room is a suit of space armour from the early twenty-first century. Suddenly it moves, pulls out a neutronsword and swings at you. You roll to the left and it hits a metal table, which breaks in half. This is no illusion. You see an array of neutronswords on display; you seize one and begin to defend yourself.

WARRIOR　　　　SKILL 9　　　　STAMINA 12

Deduct 2 TIME units. If you lose, turn to **201**; if you win, turn to **340**.

121

You find a basement to hide him and you strap on a signal unit, so that Tracebeam can find him. He snores while you cover him up with sacks. Back in the diner all eyes, including plasti-pupils, are on you. They have all realized what your profession is. Someone asks you if you got him. You turn around and see a large man wearing a T-shirt with 'Julio' on the front of it. Do you respond and chat with the man (turn to **232**), or ignore him and get on with your breakfast (turn to **335**)?

122

The Grom begins to look cross. His cheeks puff up and redden, then he vanishes. The room is plunged into darkness and you sense yourself rotating head over heels. Then you lose consciousness. Turn to **249**.

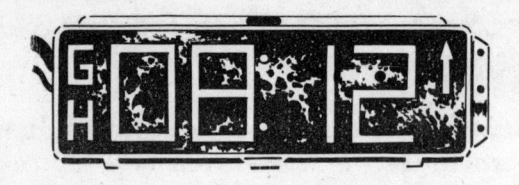

123

The Excel walks leisurely towards the palace and through the gates. There are many Guards around. One of them notices you and comes towards you. Do you retire gracefully (turn to **179**) or speak to the Guard (turn to **304**)?

124

A low whine begins, followed by *beep, beep, beep*. You realize that the alarm has gone off. The girl appears, Vidcorder in hand, but you are already on the platform and heading down. The girl is being followed by a large red balloon with a face on it; she waves to you as you disappear. Downstairs you catch sight of an Excel heading for the front door, so you run in the opposite direction. You sprint through several rooms and an open window. You forget about the beams as you rush for the outside wall. Turn to **55**.

125

You leap up on the packing-cases, reach the window and kick at the plastic grille covering it. As you prepare to launch yourself through it, a stun shot slams into your back and you are paralysed. You have no hope of finishing your mission.

126

You sit at the computer. Groms are using the plain 'L' language-system, so you call up the file directory. You ask for a visual display. A message appears, asking for a pass-code and allowing you five gravity seconds to key in. Then the screen begins to flash, 'Unauthorized User. Beware Hacker.' A low whine accompanies the flashing. Through the window you can see the Grom coming back with the Androids. As a last resort you aim a kick at the guts of the IPX. The screen goes blank and another back-up screen lights up; the tell-tale message disappears. Turn to **91**.

127

You are correct: add and subtract alternately 3, 9, 27, 81 – multiples of 3. The screen shows you a menu; you ask for current news and this gives you a sub-menu, including an item on the Galactic President. You choose this section and are asked what information you want. You key in, 'Where is the President kept?' The reply comes back, 'Not relevant to Madrid base.' You look carefully at the group supplying the information; one thing you cannot make sense of is a circle with a horizontal line through it. You know that he is not in Madrid and you must continue your search elsewhere. Turn to **169**.

128

By keeping still you have stopped its automatic hunt/kill functions. It comes up to you, knowing that its cover has been 'blown'. Under such circumstances, it is programmed to de-activate all witnesses. You manage to press the CodeMatch button and it responds immediately. It tells you that the Houlgans have damaged its disguise circuits and that it can no longer pretend that it is just a service Android. Suddenly it seizes up and falls over and you realize that it is very seriously damaged. You open up a side panel and look for damaged circuits. There are only two possible paths to follow, but you must act quickly before self-destruct sets in. Deduct 2 TIME units. Do you choose the left circuit (turn to 233) or the right circuit (turn to 375)?

129

The black knight leaps on to the left square in true chess-piece fashion; you were correct to stay still. You dodge away and jump off the board; as you run, the illusion fades and you are out on the street. You look around; there is no one to be seen. You dodge into a side-street at the sight of two GromPol craft that sweep overhead and land in the grounds of the hacienda. You check the time and realize that the Silverhound leaves soon. You rush off to catch it. Turn to 80.

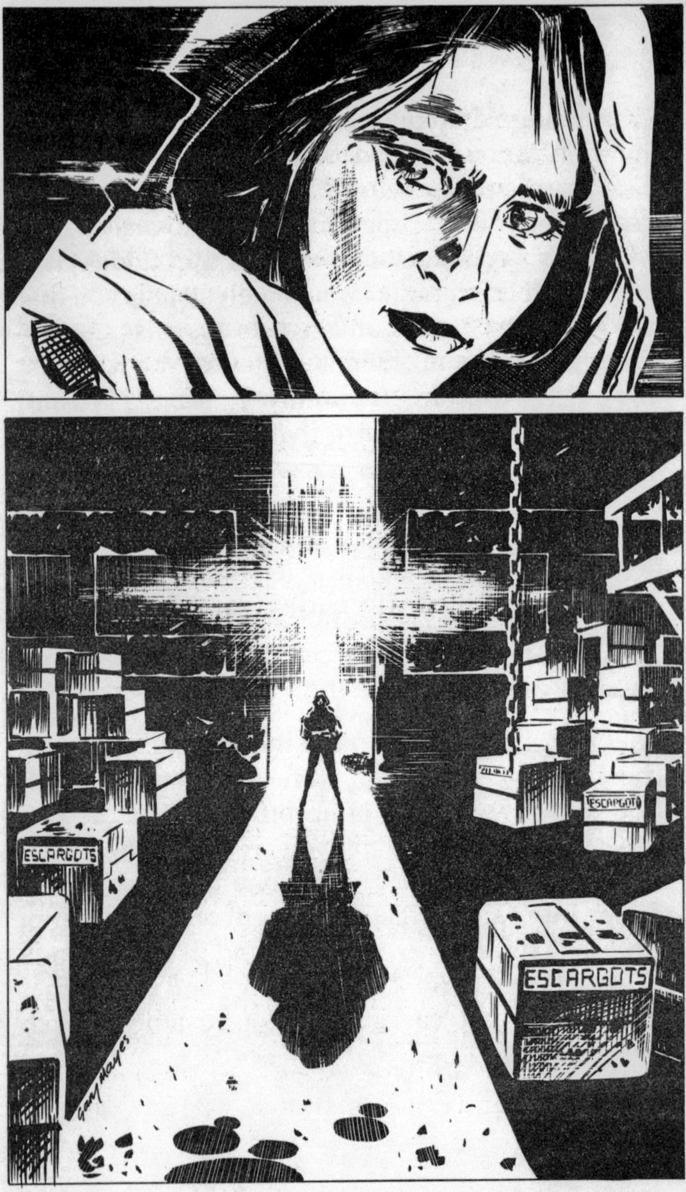
ESCARGOTS
ESCARGOT
ESCARGOTS
Gary Mayes

130

There is a crash to the left. You twist round and see the woman you came across in Roma. She clutches a Catchman and has already trussed up the rogue guard. She rushes towards you and releases you without a word. On the way out of the building you pass another rogue enveloped in plasti-net. You follow her past a big industrial transport marked 'Escargot' and she takes you to a small bar where she buys you a caffeine stimulant.

If you have not talked to her before, she introduces herself as Arana, another Rogue Tracer. She is working for the Groms, looking for some missing firmware. She tells you that she has followed some fugitives from Roma and that she intercepted your signal as she was passing the warehouse. She has to rush off, but directs you towards two Grom base stations: one to the north (turn to 356) and one to the south (turn to 204).

131

You are in a chamber that looks as though it was built four hundred gravity years ago. It is collapsing around you: large segments of concrete fall from the roof in random order. Roll one die: this is your position. Roll the second die: this is where a slab falls. If the two numbers are the same, you are crushed. Repeat this procedure four times. If you survive, there are blocked exits to the south and north-west, and exits east (turn to 353) or west (turn to 44).

132

Your companion explains everything to the rest of the gang outside the food bar. You let them know that you are a Rogue Tracer working against the Groms. They seem to despise Groms as much as rival Houlgan gangs. You all enter the bar, where they order strange-sounding food. When it arrives there are no cubes, but a mass of small sea-creatures immersed in yellow grains. You fear contamination and are at first reluctant to eat, but the smell is so wonderful that you cannot resist. The food turns out to be even better than your mother's home-made food cubes. Add 3 STAMINA points. Turn to 315.

133

The landing is bad. You have broken both of your legs and you cannot move. The Groms spot you and come down to pick you up. You will not recover in time to complete your mission.

134

You make your way to the Silverhound terminal. Before you go in, you see a squad of GromPols and a sign flashing above them announcing, 'All services are cancelled.' You back out and catch sight of a bank of Vidscreens; they have stopped showing ads and are transmitting pictures of you. As you head back to the transport craft you saw earlier, you come across another in the process of refuelling. It is also full of crates marked with a circle and horizontal line. Do you try getting on to this craft (turn to **245**), or will you go back to the other one (turn to **239**)?

135

The Android walks towards the building and you watch carefully as it approaches one of the Guards at the door. The Guard takes out its stun gun and looks towards you. Suddenly you remember that some Androids are equipped with sense-detect and know when anyone is following them. You dive into the bushes. A tree beside you explodes and you see a GromPol craft flying towards you, cannons firing. Above the clamour and rocket whine a steely voice orders you to stay where you are. Do you do as ordered (turn to **30**), or take a chance and run for it (turn to **244**)?

136

You carry on, but the road becomes very overgrown and you lose your direction. Just then you see a Grom standing with his back to you. He has picked up a small snail and is in the process of inserting it into his ear. You notice that his other ear already has a small shell protruding from it. You decide to take a risk and ask him for directions to the general area you are seeking. He cannot hear you (because he's got snail shells in his ears), so you tap him on the shoulder. Suddenly two Guards appear and grab you. The Grom turns around, greatly agitated, and tells you that you are under arrest for touching a Gromulan. He stumbles off, leaving you with the Androids. Do you put up a fight (turn to **399**) or go quietly (turn to **168**)?

137

You begin to realize the error you made in stealing the craft. You have blown your cover and your Rogue Tracer ID is logged in the central IPX computer. You look up and notice three craft taking off and disappearing into the distance. You assume that they believe you to have perished in the crash. You destroy your original ID and redraft a new one on your Chronograph, hoping that no Vidgraph has been secretly taken of your face. You walk down a slope and come to a track running north to south. Will you go north (turn to 363) or south (turn to 256)?

138

You want to ask the fugitives a few questions, but they speak a dialect that your Transinterpreter cannot understand. You stash them for later collection and go downstairs. Deduct 2 TIME units and turn to 295.

139

You are in a chamber with a blocked exit east, but other exits south (turn to 331) or west (turn to 62). There is also an exit north, which slopes down and you can see that water has flooded it. Occasionally, strange-fanged fish break the surface and snap ferociously at one another. If you wish to go this way, turn to 384.

140

You will have to leap from building to building. Roll two dice and add up the total: this is the first distance to leap. Roll one die and add the result to your STAMINA score: this is your first jump. If your jump is equal to or greater than the distance, then you have successfully jumped to the next building. Repeat this three times. If at any time the distance is greater than the jump, you have fallen to your death. If you succeed, deduct 2 STAMINA points. You have got to the fourth building and found access down to the street. Turn to 79.

141

You let him win and take care not to give yourself away by your style of fighting. He accepts you into the group. He is proud of the fact that he has beaten everyone in the gang. He slaps you on the back and tells you that he will test you out on a plum job: 'The hacienda – lots of rich pickings there.' He tells you that it is the residence of a highly placed Grom. It appears that although Earth is a haven from Tracebeam, it is difficult to make ends meet without leaving the planet. You are given some food cubes. Add 1 STAMINA point. After several gravity hours, a guide and adviser takes you along the sewers to the hacienda. Turn to **273**.

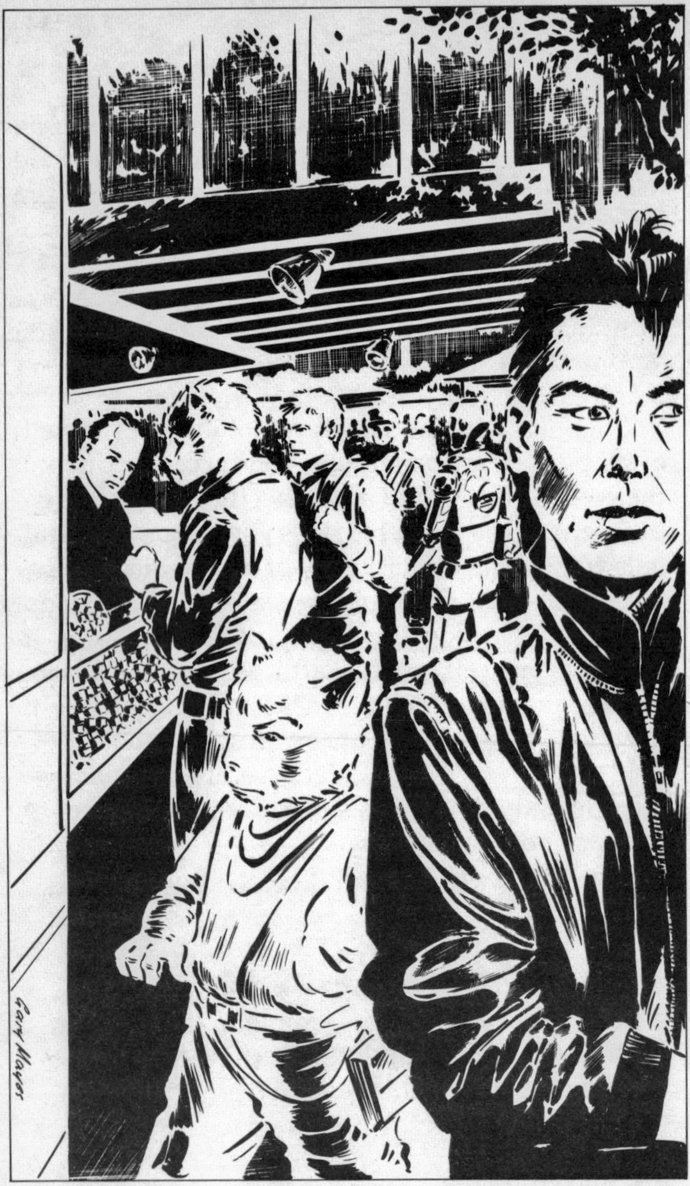
Gary Mayes

142

You walk through a maze of narrow streets until you come to a market. Most people are selling food cubes and among the customers are Felines from Wistas 4. You feel the CodeMatch on your Chronograph activate as an Android passes you, carrying a parcel. You follow carefully. You know that you are running out of time. Deduct 2 TIME units. Do you approach the Android (turn to 198), or do you prefer not to trust it and carry on alone (turn to 221)?

143

You are right to be suspicious. The craft is a disguised Bandit ZipCar out for plunder. Your car is no great speedster, but the cannons are loaded. Fight as in ordinary combat, but do not reduce your actual STAMINA, since it is the craft which takes damage. Use a SPECIAL Encounter Box on the Adventure Sheet.

BANDIT ZIPCAR   SKILL 7   STAMINA 8

If you lose, you have crashed, but you survive and run off into a nearby trench which seems to head back to the city (turn to 3). If you win, turn to 302.

144

You are in White room, Level 3. Reduce OXYGEN by 1 unit. There is one door leading up (turn to 181), a door on the left leading down (turn to 352) and a door on the right leading down (turn to 284).

145

You stand around and watch the bus take off. The waiting bores you, and you find a door marked 'Private'. It is open and you go in to find an empty office with a notice lying on the floor, which tells you that all Rocket-a-Hire services have been cancelled due to lack of demand. You look through a small window at the Sweepertron, which is heading towards you. Just then two GromPol Androids appear and block its path. Suddenly steam rises from its face and it begins to melt in self-destruct mode. You realize that the Sweepertron was one of your contacts! Turn to **99**.

146

You are in Violet room, Level 3. Reduce OXYGEN by 1 unit. There is one door leading up (turn to **97**) and another leading down (turn to **377**).

147

You realize that credits might be a good way to get their help. As you reach for your cards, one of the smallest of them rushes past you and grabs the whole pack out of your hands. You pull out your Catchman and the others scatter in all directions. You aim for the thief. Throw a die: if you throw 3 or under, your gun has jammed (turn to **231**); if you throw 4 or above, you have ensnared him (turn to **345**).

148

You have heard alarm sirens in the distance and now you arrive at a thick metal door. There is no way through. Fifty metres behind you, another door has shut. You feel the air being drained from the tunnel. Your mission has failed.

149

The conveyor moves at a good pace and you notice the rough-hewn tunnel change to a metal-clad one. You guess that you are close to the city centre when you see a light ahead. There is a huge machine attended by several Androids. You get off and walk carefully along the tunnel, but there are no Guards here. The Androids are 'dedicated' and blind to anything but their own function. Deduct 2 TIME units. There are two ladders heading straight up. Do you take the left one (turn to **344**) or the right one (turn to **329**)?

150

You check the motor and fuel levels, close the hood and open the plexi-glass cockpit cover. You see that the ZipCar is full of hot, bubbling mud. As you peer closer four hands reach out of the mud towards you; at the end of each finger is a bloody claw. *Test your Fear Factor*. If you are frightened, reduce your STAMINA by 1 point. Deduct 2 TIME units and turn to **261**.

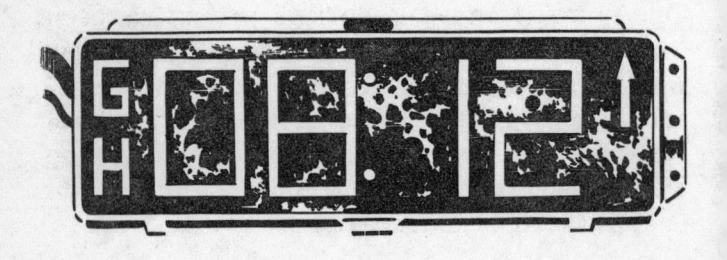

151

Arana gives you good directions. The road is broad and clear and there seem to be more Groms walking around, although they are always accompanied by Guards, who walk particularly slowly, to let their short-legged masters keep up with them. The Roxyrama is an old Vid Palace set up in the days before Illus-o-Vision 70, when 3-D entertainment had to take place in special buildings. It looks shut when you get there. You pull at a metal grille and step inside. Deduct 2 TIME units. Do you go along the corridor (turn to **295**) or up the staircase (turn to **362**)?

152

The Android wanders off out of the terminal. You give it a few minutes and then go to the window. You look out carefully. It is speaking to two Grom-Pol Androids and it is obvious that it has been 'turned'. Luckily the planted Androids do not know what you look like. The 'turned' Android moves off and fingers its stun gun as it passes a group of Houlgans who are trying to break in to a food-cube dispenser. Do you follow the Android (turn to **238**) or approach the Houlgans (turn to **29**)?

153

She moves very fast and seems to know instinctively that you are following her. Roma is busier than Madrid, with a few more natives visible. You follow at speed, but are suddenly halted by a solid arm. A GromPol wants to check your ID, so you have to stop to show it. *Test your Luck*. If you are Lucky, you manage to catch up with her (turn to **298**). If you are Unlucky, you have lost her (turn to **221**).

154

The owner is a rough-looking type. You look in and see that the ZipCar has several extra cannons fitted. You ask him if he is heading north and if he is willing to give you a lift. He looks you up and down and agrees. You get into the back and he takes off. He stays at cruising speed and ahead you can see the Silverhound in the distance. He asks you your business. Do you tell the truth (turn to **247**) or tell him that you are a trader (turn to **86**)?

155

You are wise not to trust the Groms. Your missile hits the Dragon and causes a mega-explosion. The creature was a missile with an Illus-o-Scope on board. The rescue craft speeds off to the mother ship and the fleet. Turn to **400**.

156

A cannon shot explodes close to you. You weave and dodge into a half-demolished building across the street. The Gromulan craft fires its cannons again and you feel the floor give way, just before you black out. Turn to **313**.

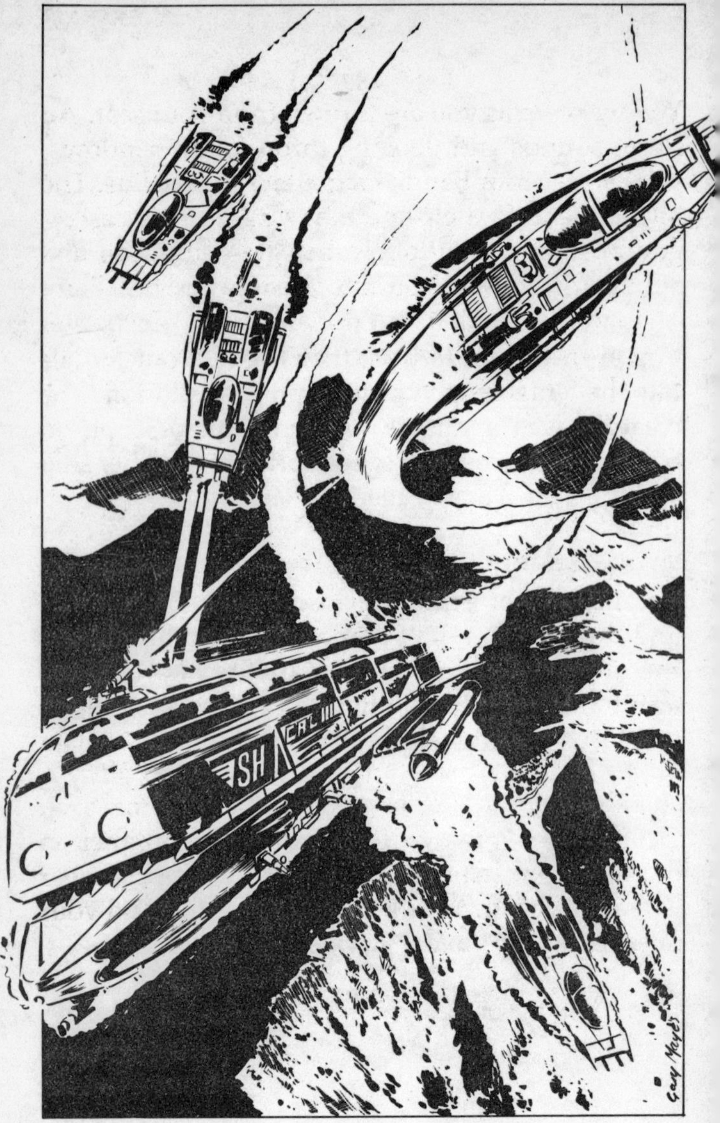
SH

157

You wake up as you are thrown from your seat. An alarm sounds and, looking through the windows, you can see four Bandit craft attacking the bus. The pilot appeals for help and the two Androids rush to gun positions. You follow and grab a cannon that appears on a pivot. You aim carefully and fire. Fight as in normal combat, but use a SPECIAL Encounter Box on your *Adventure Sheet*, and do not reduce your actual STAMINA score.

	SKILL	STAMINA
First BANDIT	9	8
Second BANDIT	9	10

If you lose, turn to **269**. If you win, turn to **227**.

158

You are in the laser-welding room. There are six chambers, full of Androids, and lasers are firing at them in random order from across the room. You cannot go back, so you have to go past the six chambers to the exit. Throw one die for each chamber in sequence. If at any time the number on the die is the same as the number of the chamber you are passing, then you have been hit, and your mission is over. If you survive, turn to **348**.

159

A stop is announced for breakfast. The Silverhound sets down in a craft-park by a small diner. This is no galactic service-station; a sign proudly proclaims: 'Julio's: under original Earthling management'. You follow the others inside. There is a wide selection of food cubes and drink tubes for sale. While you tug at a tube, you turn around and come face to face with Kinta Lopsti, an escaped prisoner whom you originally arrested. He recognizes you and rushes out of the door. Do you give chase (turn to **299**) or keep a low profile and let him go (turn to **17**)?

160

Deduct 2 TIME units. The door slides open. You see an Android sitting at a ComTerm. It turns around and raises a stun gun towards you. You strike immediately and kick the gun out of its clutch.

TECHNICAL
OPERATOR   SKILL 6   STAMINA 8

If you win, turn to **317**.

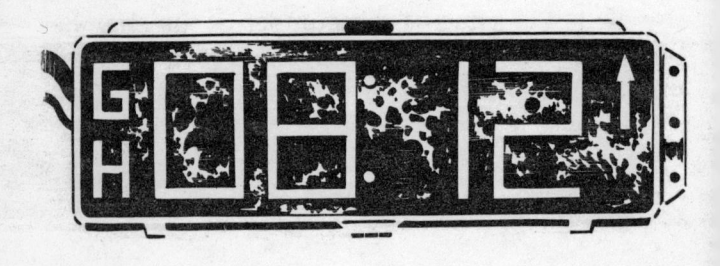

161

The people thank you for your help. You ask the girl behind the bar if you can borrow the Mark I ZipCar. She agrees and asks you to leave it in the bus terminal to be picked up by a relative. She gives you the settings and some food cubes. Add 1 STAMINA point. Turn to **280**.

162

They follow you as you splash along. After a while you turn around and notice that they have stopped and are staring at something behind you. You look in the same direction and see the flashing lights and laser blasts of a Grom Rodent Killer. It moves along the tunnel blasting at any living thing. You run back and find that the others have disappeared. You take the right fork. Turn to **73**.

163

You sit at the controls. The craft rises and you put your foot down. The speed of acceleration pushes you into the soft seat. As the ship gains height you notice a small flashing light and realize that it had needed to take on fuel! You have forgotten that phozon is not available on Earth and they still rely on things like fuel gauges. The craft suddenly loses power and drops. You push the ejectormatic, knowing that your luck must be in for one of these to work efficiently. *Test your Luck*. If you are Unlucky, turn to **191**. If you are Lucky, turn to **222**.

164

As you move towards the bushes, you feel the slap of a stun shot on your chest. You are only winded, but you are dealing with a high-quality, state-of-the-art Excel Android. You reel backwards and it is upon you. It has moved two hundred metres in a few gravity seconds. Turn to **366**.

165

Orvium orders the body to be thrown out. He tells you that you are brave, but that he suspects you are from the galactic centre. You tell him that you want the Grom firmware and Galaxy One is willing to pay a high price. He wants to know how high and stresses that it is up to date and unprotected. You ask to see it and he gives you thirty gravity seconds in front of it. They take you to an old IPX. You flip through the menus until you get to information about the President. With several seconds left, you have a choice of two buttons for his location. Do you press button A (turn to **38**) or button B (turn to **297**)?

166

You have opened the correct door. Add 2 LUCK points. It opens into daylight outside an old high wall. You cannot believe that the Groms have let you go – and then you look to either side of you. Two Excels in ritual duelling armour stand with neutronswords raised above their heads. The beams swish downwards. You drop flat on to the ground. When you look up, you see that one of the Excels has a deep gash through its chest-piece and, while you watch, it falls over in a cloud of acidic self-destruct. The other Excel has lost its right arm. They have missed you and hit each other! The remaining Android comes at you.

ONE-ARMED
  EXCEL   SKILL 4   STAMINA 4

If you lose, you have no excuses. If you win, turn to 328.

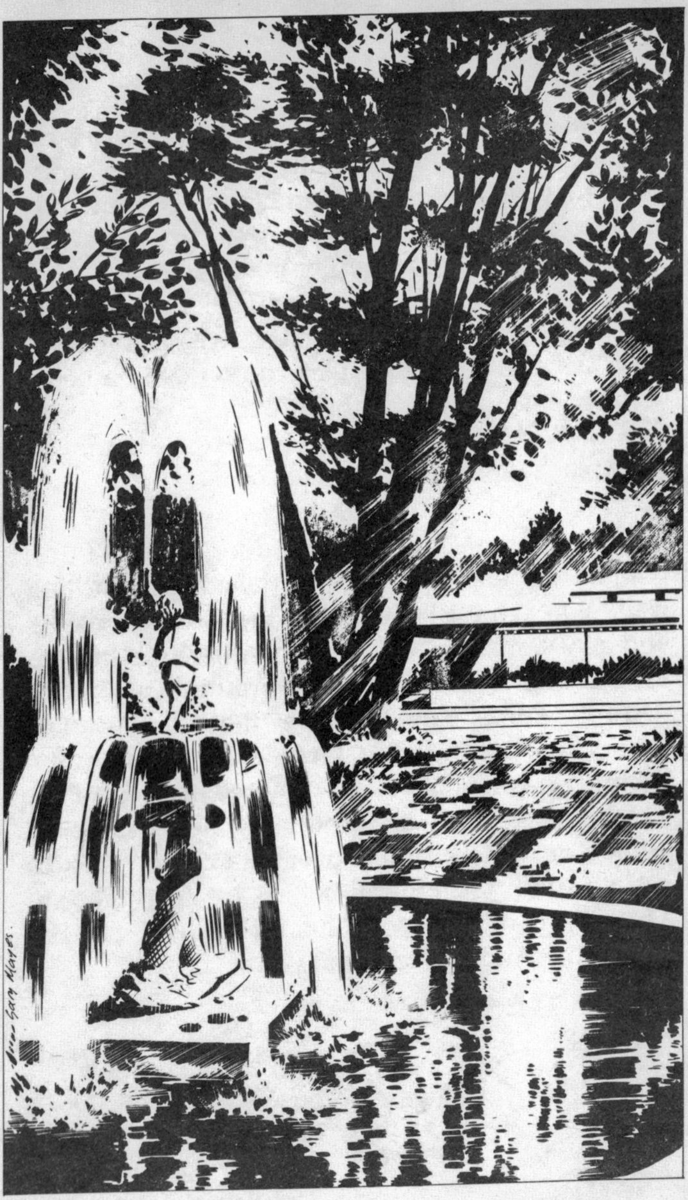

167

The building is spacious and luxurious. There is no one around and you carefully slip into the courtyard. Just then a gust of wind blows up some dust and reveals beams criss-crossing the open space in random order. You carefully make your way. Deduct 2 TIME units. Throw one die: this is where the beam is. Throw a second die: this is where you move to. If the two throws match, you have hit a beam (turn to 55). Repeat this procedure three more times. If you succeed without breaking a beam, you have reached the door (turn to 100).

168

You are marched off to a nearby Grom craft and thrown into a small dark cell. After several gravity hours you feel the craft take off. Soon you are taken into a building marked 'Bastille' and lined up in a corridor with a row of other criminals. Androids clatter up and down looking busy. In the far corner there is a door marked 'Communications – Private'. You watch carefully when a Grom comes out, and you see a ComTerm inside. Do you risk going in (turn to 10), or will you stay where you are (turn to 110)?

169

You make your way back downstairs. The sound of blasters and stun guns has stopped. The elevator door opens and there is Gus, practically torn apart. In front of Gus lie bits of four Guards, dripping fluid over the shiny floor. You help Gus out of the building, but the poor Android can hardly stand. It senses other Guards arriving and tells you to get off to the Silverhound terminal, since you have very little time to catch the bus for Roma. Gus prepares to hold the Guards off to give you a chance to escape. You run off towards the terminal. Deduct 2 TIME units. Turn to **80**.

170

You walk up to the ZipCar. It really is an antique: a Zip Fordos, single rocket, manual drive. It is easy for a trained Rogue Tracer to break into, but as you finger the handle a steely voice screams at you, 'You, you're a dead man!' The voice seems to come from inside the hotel. Do you run (turn to **77**) or turn around with your hands up and enter the hotel (turn to **197**)?

171

Lopsti notices that you are unattended and slaps your guard across the face. Turn to **95**.

172

The black knight leaps on top of you. You have moved into its path. You feel dizzy and fall down. The illusion fades and you are surrounded by three Excels. They do not mess around: this is the end of your mission.

173

The blaster, set at maximum, punches a hole through the Guard, which collapses and self-destructs. Before you can reset, the Excel is upon you.

EXCEL   SKILL 12   STAMINA 16

If you win, turn to **34**.

174

They put their heads together. When they come back, the leader tells you that they will take you to their hideout. They lead off at a fast pace and turn into a maze of small alleyways which even your trained mind cannot keep track of. Suddenly one of the gang whistles and they all take off in various directions. You catch sight of three of them, but which one do you chase:

The one ahead in the alley?	Turn to **46**
The one to the left in a doorway?	Turn to **271**
The one to the right in a doorway?	Turn to **393**

175

You go, with them leading the way out. Delicately you pull out your Catchman, turn and fire at the first three gang members. Roll one die: if you throw 3 or under, the gun has jammed (turn to **248**); if you throw 4 or over, the Catchman works (turn to **84**).

176

He leads you out of the Roxyrama. He takes giant strides and you try to keep up with him. The road is deserted, overgrown and full of ruins. At one crossroads he stops, pulls out a blaster and carefully edges round the corner. Just then a Grom task-force rockets in; they retro down from roofs and out of windows. Your companion starts firing and rushes at a group: he knocks down three with one blow. A Grom craft is directing operations from high above. Do you join in the fight (turn to **210**) or try to slip away (turn to **305**)?

177

You cannot believe your eyes. You have come across an old Vidprint from the time of the Groms' first arrival on Earth, detailing all their civic works, and including various plans. You quickly glance through the document on the shop's viewer. The Grom main administrative base is built under the Ents Complex at the Plaza de Toros. Senior Groms live in large haciendas; the nearest is quite close to where you are. Add 2 LUCK points. Do you head for the Plaza de Toros (turn to **390**) or the hacienda (turn to **246**)?

178

The ZipCar comes down fast and plunges deep into a salt lake. The ejectormatic does not work. You've had it.

179

You make your way towards the Silverhound terminal. A few natives wander around, carrying heavy cases. In the craft-park there are two buses, one marked ROMA and the other being repaired by a team of Mechnoids. You see a sign marked 'Services' and head towards it. Turn to **235**.

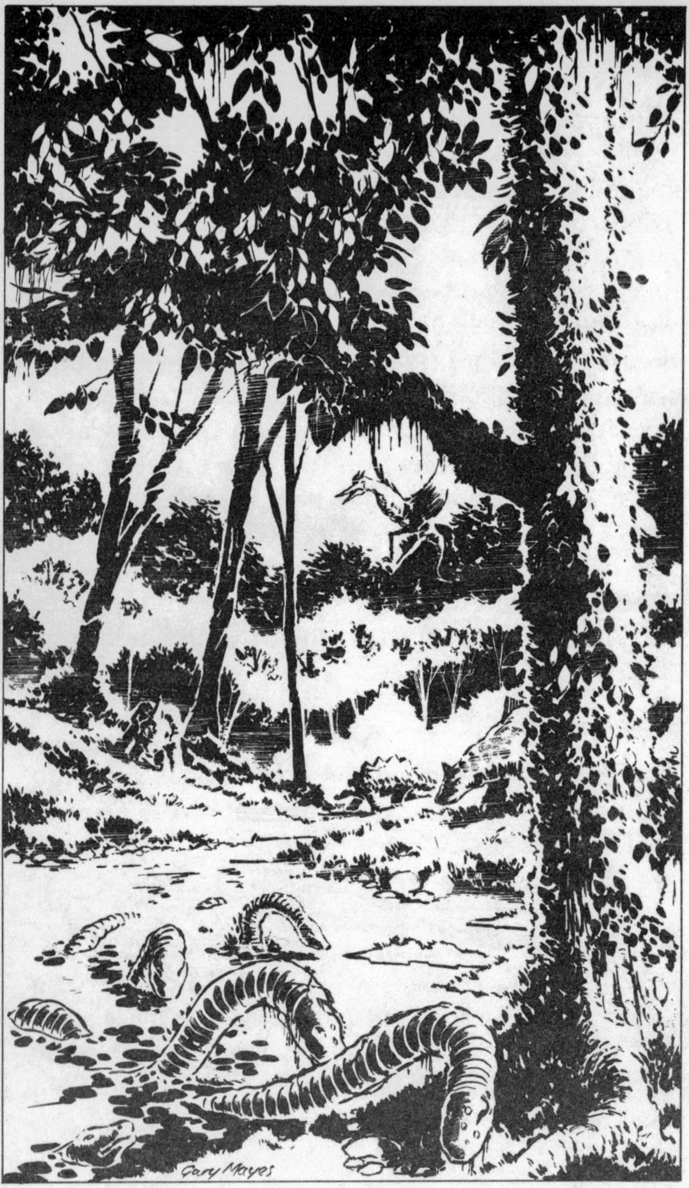
Gary Mayes

180

You are enveloped in a prehistoric forest, full of strange creatures. The ground is a swamp with snake-like creatures slithering through it. All the exits are hidden from you. This is no mere illusion but a full-scale Grom reproduction. You make no headway on your speedboard, so you abandon it and start hacking through the undergrowth with the neutronsword. It is impossible to tell the best way to go. Will you choose:

Heading A?	Turn to 320
Heading B?	Turn to 220
Heading C?	Turn to 359

181

You are in Blue room, Level 2. Reduce OXYGEN by 1 unit. There is one door leading up (turn to 51), one door on the left leading down (turn to 215) and one door on the right leading down (turn to 144).

182

When you regain consciousness, you are facing the Grom. The craft is speeding along. The Grom smiles and expresses his apologies. He has checked your ID with base station and it matches information about known Rogue Tracers. He asks you if you play chess and you agree to a game. Immediately a beautiful set appears suspended in mid-air. He tells you that they will be making a stop first, but will get you back to the bus as soon as possible. You find him to be very intelligent and galaxy-wise. He wins the game easily.

The craft settles in a GromPol station. You stay in the craft and watch the Grom, who is talking to two Guards outside and pointing towards you. In front of you is a standard IPX computer. Do you trust the Grom, sit back and relax (turn to **270**), take the opportunity of getting information from the computer (turn to **126**), or steal the GromPol craft and fly away (turn to **163**)?

183

They lead you to the building by various backstreets. They are cautious, because this is not their territory. They place scouts along the route and signals are passed along the line. They lead you to the service entrance of the hacienda, shake hands and retreat in orderly fashion. You check your Chronograph and have a good look at the building. Turn to **167**.

184

Your Chronograph shows that you have twenty-five seconds before your pursuers begin the chase. You realize that you don't know the country and that Rocket Bikes have a very limited range. You look around you: to the left are smooth brown mountains and to the right is a forested valley. Deduct 2 TIME units. Do you head left (turn to 294) or right (turn to 391)?

185

You reach the door but cannot open it: there is no handle, grip or button. You turn around. The ground trembles and the bull is almost upon you. You decide to dodge left, but you leave it very late. *Test your Luck*. If you are Lucky, you get away with a grazed side. Reduce your STAMINA by 1 point and turn to 111. If you are Unlucky, farewell, brave matador!

186

You tell Orvium that you'll be back in two gravity hours. As you leave, however, you come face to face with Brak 9 and two grubby Excel Androids. Brak, an old pirate now in semi-retirement, recognizes you and sets the Excels to hold you while he calls Orvium over and tells him of your Rogue Tracer status. Orvium punches you and you collapse. Turn to 313.

187

After half a gravity hour you begin to give up hope. But then there is a crash to the left. You twist round and see an Android, stun gun in hand, standing over your guard. It rushes over and releases you without a word, and you follow it into the street. Outside the building stands a large industrial transport craft marked 'Escargot'. When the Android thinks that you are safe, it stops, points to a doorway and tells you to go in. It will return soon with important information about the President. Do you go into the building (turn to 300) or not (turn to 98)?

188
You are stuck, with no transport. You have missed the bus in all senses of the phrase. You have failed in your mission.

189
You are in Indigo room, Level 4. Reduce OXYGEN by 1 unit. There is one door leading up. Turn to **215**.

190
You are right to take no notice of the screen. An Excel is watching you from a distant corner of the garden. The Grom returns and announces that his Android will give you a lift to Madrid in his launch. Turn to **382**.

191
The ejectormatic does not function and you smash the craft into the ground.

192

There are bars that stick out, but each one is further than you can reach. You will have to leap and catch each bar. Roll three dice: the total is the first distance to leap. Roll one die and add the number to your STAMINA score: this is your first leap. If your leap is equal to or greater than the distance, then you have successfully jumped. If not, you have fallen down the shaft to your death. Repeat this procedure three more times. If you reach the top, reduce your STAMINA by 1 point and turn to **209**.

193

You decide to stay with Willi, since you reckon that its knowledge of the building is greater than yours. You both walk for a gravity hour; the passage remains dark, damp and rather smelly. Willi's limp gets worse and soon its light begins to fade. Then the light goes out and Willi collapses in a heap. You smell the pungent odour of self-destruct, but can see nothing. You turn back. *Test your Luck*. If you are Lucky, you have found your way back to the ladder (turn to **25**). If you are Unlucky, you are doomed to wander around until you also drop down dead.

194

You go through the door marked EXIT. Alarm lights are flashing and you hear the door lock itself behind you. A screen to the left prints a message:

LIFE FORM ACCESS. EXPEL OXYGEN FROM ALL AREAS IN 20 UNITS.

Mark the 20 units in the OXYGEN box on your *Adventure Sheet* and make deductions as instructed. If the units reach zero, you can no longer breathe and your mission is over. Turn to **51**.

195

The explosion shatters the ground and you fall into a chamber. You get up, slightly bruised, and look around. The only exit is a tunnel with water rushing through it. There is a faint light from small airshafts. As you wade upstream, the tunnel divides. Do you go left (turn to **372**) or right (turn to **202**)?

196

You are in Green room, Level 3. Deduct 1 OXYGEN unit. There is a door leading up (turn to **97**), a door to the left leading down (turn to **272**) and a door to the right leading down (turn to **392**).

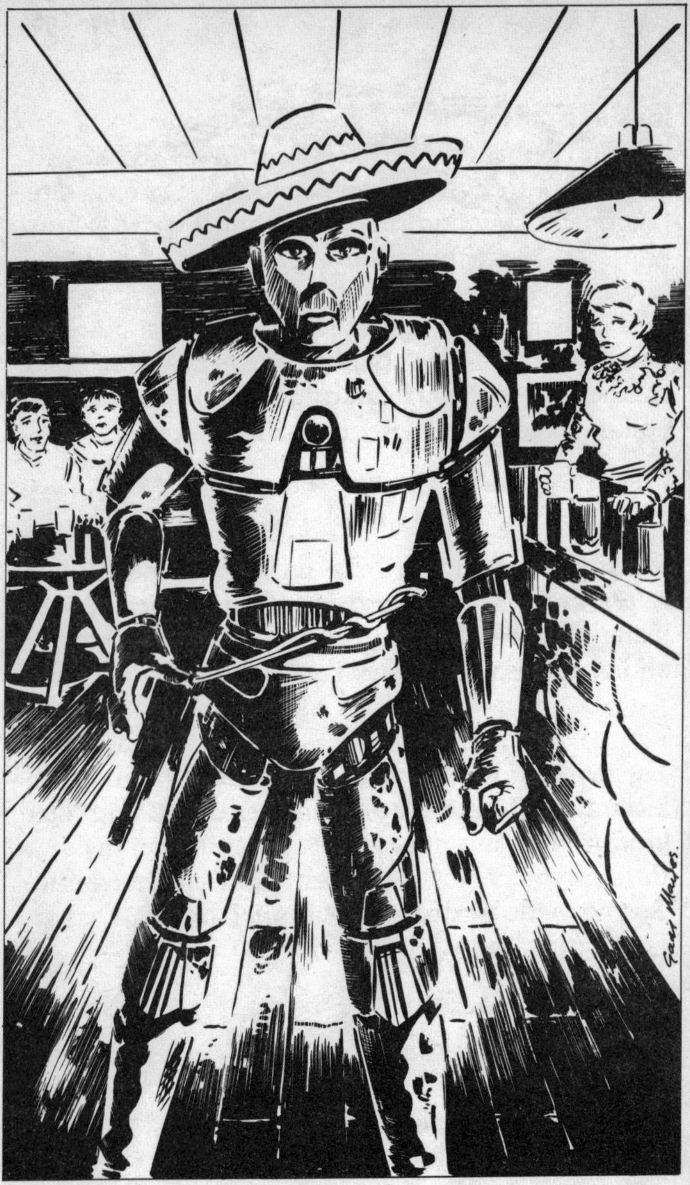

197

Inside the Alcazar, you see a couple of men, a girl behind the bar and an Excel Android. Excels, with their supreme fighting ability and their strength, are the most dangerous of all the Grom Androids. This one is wearing a funny hat. It has placed its stun gun low on its 'hip' and is facing you with its arm slightly raised. You notice that the stun gun is set at maximum killing power. 'Draw,' its speech circuits rumble. Do you pull out your Catchman (turn to **277**) or try to talk to it (turn to **50**)?

198

You catch up and press CodeMatch. The Android does not respond, but walks on. You follow. It stops at a service bay and plugs in some lubricant. You stand near and it begins to talk without looking at you. It tells you that it is suspected and that you will have to act quickly to get any information. It tells you of two options. There is a Grom sub-station near by that is sure to have records; or you could travel to the salt-mines where the President was brought down, to see if you can discover any evidence there. Will you go to the sub-station (turn to **257**) or the salt-mines (turn to **108**)?

199

You must look after yourself. You do not know when you will next get the chance to eat. Reduce your STAMINA by 1 point. Turn to **39**.

200

You get to the Plaza de Toros and stand by a high wall. Willi goes off to check a side door into the Ents Complex. Suddenly you feel a stabbing pain in your left shoulder (lose 1 STAMINA point). You twist round, pulling out your Catchman and dropping to the ground. In front of you stands Horit Lam, a former Rogue Tracer and now a fugitive from justice. You fire your Catchman, but your aim is not true and the plasti-net envelops his stun gun. He is upon you before you can fire again. As you struggle, you can see Willi in the distance holding up a manhole and waving. Do you fight (turn to **341**) or run away (turn to **13**)?

201

When your eyes can focus, you find yourself sitting at a table facing a small, middle-aged Grom. He greets you as 'one of the famous Rogue Tracers', and returns your ID to you. He admits that he was bored and that he conjured up the 'entertainment' on the spur of the moment. He then asks you what you want. You tell him that you are heading for Madrid. He smiles and tells you that he has a launch on the river, if you are willing to play for it. A chess set appears. 'Of course,' he adds, 'if you lose, you die.' Behind you stands an Excel and you have no real choice whether or not to play. Use your SKILL score and substitute CUNNING for your STAMINA score. Play the game as in normal combat, but use a SPECIAL Encounter Box of the *Adventure Sheet* and do not reduce your actual STAMINA score.

GROM   SKILL 10   CUNNING 10

If you win, you are taken to his launch (turn to **382**). If you lose, the Excel hits you (turn to **40**).

202

You stagger along for a while until you see a light ahead. You find another collapsed roof, but it is very high. There is a thick metal grille blocking the rest of the tunnel. Do you try to leap up to the hole (turn to **229**), or will you go back and take the left-hand fork (turn to **372**)?

203

A good idea. You will need all your energy when you are on the planet. Add 1 STAMINA point. Turn to **39**.

204

You walk south along a wide avenue which leads to a bridge over a dusty expanse that must have once been a river. You are tired, hungry and thirsty. You notice some people entering a bar across the road, called 'Le Spot'. Do you go in and fortify yourself (turn to **14**) or carry on (turn to **136**)?

205

You approach the Excel cautiously. You know that Groms always build disabling points in all their Androids, since they fear their creations turning against them. You try to find the weak spot. Throw two dice: if you throw double 6, you have found it (turn to **161**); otherwise, turn to **277**.

206

You know the power of the Excel Androids: they have high-quality vision, speed, power and intelligence. You are wise to put up no resistance. It covers the two hundred metres in a few seconds. Turn to 366.

207

You are in the alley. There are paths in all four directions but you do not know which way to head. You decide to climb to the top of the nearest building to have a look around. You climb a rickety wooden staircase to the top of the roof. The building is gutted on the inside. From up here you can see the way back to the open avenues, but when you get back to the staircase you find that it has collapsed. You suspect the Houlgans. The distance between buildings is not great and you think that you could jump to the next building. Turn to 140.

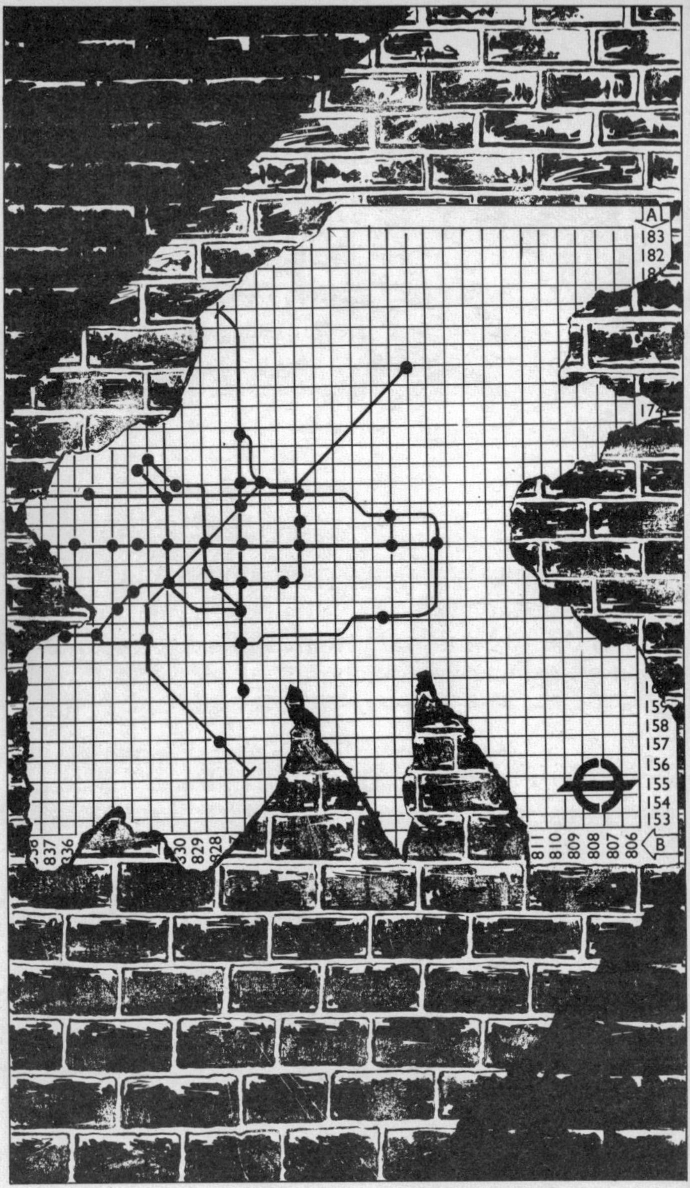
A
183
182
158
157
156
155
154
153
B
837
830
829
828
811
810
809
808
807
806

208

The Chronograph wakes you up just as the transport is landing. You get up and stroll through an open hatch. A robot ignores you as it unloads the crates. You look around, but see nothing except a bleak wasteland. The only feature is a tunnel entrance into which the crates are being conveyed. There is a sign above the entrance: a circle with a horizontal line through it. You walk into the tunnel and to your left you see an old poster stuck on a brick wall. Add 4 LUCK points.

Study the poster carefully and use any clues you have acquired in your travels. You are at the southernmost point of the tunnel system. Keep this page marked, since you will have to refer back to work out your relative position.

You walk into the tunnel until you come to a small chamber stacked with crates. The tunnel continues in a north-westerly direction. Beside the crates you see a sophisticated speedboard with several attachments, including an old-fashioned neutronsword. Do you jump on and take it (turn to 274) or approach carefully to see if anyone is around (turn to 323)?

209

Eventually you reach the top. You stand on a small platform and glare at a heavy metal grille. There is no way of forcing it. You look around carefully and discover a crack in the wall opposite the grille. You follow the crack all the way round, until you come to a metal ring hidden by the dust. A door opens when you twist the ring, and you step out, exhausted, and look around. The door shuts behind you with a soft clunk. Turn to 342.

210

You leap forward and he hands you one of his blasters. You follow him through ranks of Androids, which seem to be no match for him, but just then the Grom craft drops a catch-all plasti-net, which envelops everybody in a sticky, smelly mess. You are caught and will be held for many days. You cannot succeed in your mission.

211

You set the craft on the route to Madrid. Do you proceed with caution, keeping visuals from horizon to horizon (turn to 321), or will you get some sleep while the craft is on auto-pilot (turn to 240)?

212

Turn to 23.

213

As you dash across the road, you feel a stun shot pass over your shoulder. Suddenly a manhole opens in the middle of the road and someone fires back at the Android. He calls you over and you dive into the tunnel. He shuts it and seals it with a shot from his stun gun. You follow him through a waste system. He eventually opens a large metal door which leads off to a series of rooms full of men and women who are very familiar to you from 'wanted' Vids. This is a real rogues' gallery. Turn to 4.

214

You hope to confuse it and slow it down. The beer is obviously having a strange effect on its workings. It stops whirring and tells you that its horse, a creature which you know is extinct, is outside. You look out and there is a horse! You realize that it also has a built-in Illus-o-Scope. Then the Android drops its gun and attacks you.

EXCEL COWBOY   SKILL 10   STAMINA 12

If you win, turn to 161.

215

You are in Orange room, Level 3. Reduce OXYGEN by 1 unit. There is a door leading up (turn to 181), a door leading down to the left (turn to 189) and a door leading down to the right (turn to 397).

216

You beat him easily, but everyone recognizes the Rogue Tracer style of fighting and a mass of them jump on you. They take you away and get rid of you. Needless to say, your mission is over.

217

Deduct 2 TIME units. The alarm siren wakes you up and, startled, you see a message coming through on your screen:

NO UNAUTHORIZED CROSS-CHANNEL TRAFFIC.
DANGER: RADIOACTIVE AREA.

Do you take the risk (turn to **118**) or turn back for Paris (turn to **78**)?

218

You are taken to see the Grom in charge. He is small and fat, and sits with his back to you, playing chess with his IPX. As he turns around his image changes; he seems taller, stronger and better-looking. You know that it's just an illusion. He tells you that they are after Orvium and that if you can trace him, you will be well rewarded. You agree and are escorted to the other side of the roadblock. The road to Gino's takes you through a bleak urban landscape. Turn to **370**.

219

Back on the bus the others stare at you. The Silverhound takes off and hurtles along, a hundred metres above the old Earth highway. As the sun begins to rise you notice the landscape. The Grom ahead is watching an episode from the latest Galactic Ents 'soap' on his private Vidscreen. The hard-sell commercials continue on the screen in front of you. Deduct 2 TIME units. Turn to **159**.

220

You cut your way through the undergrowth. Once, when you happen to look up, you see a metal ladder going straight up. You climb this and find yourself in a tunnel going north-west. As you walk along, random and irregular parts of the floor open up and shut. From the flames and heat below you realize that you'll have to watch your step. Throw one die: this is the section that has opened. Throw a second die: this is where you are standing. If the first number is the same as the second, you have fallen into the fiery furnace. Repeat this procedure three more times. If you survive, turn to **278**.

221

You wander around the streets, but see nothing to help you in your task. Eventually, you see a Grom, who is accompanied by two Guards. You follow at a distance; they are conducting some kind of survey. Reckoning that the Grom must lead you to a Com-Term some time, you stay on their trail. They reach a huge steel-mesh gate, open it up, go through and disappear into the deserted side-streets. Deduct 2 TIME units. Do you want to go over the gate and follow them (turn to **66**), or will you return to the bus terminal (turn to **75**)?

222

The ejectormatic works and you get shot out of the craft and retro-ed down by the rockets on the back of your seat. You land with a bump. *Test your Luck*. If you are Lucky, turn to **330**; if you are Unlucky, turn to **133**.

223
You obey Willi instinctively and hide behind the ComTerm. Willi greets the Guards in a friendly manner, but they are suspicious. When they go for their stun guns, Willi moves at tremendous speed, touches the left one on a spot on its side, and the other at the back of its neck. They both de-activate with a hiss. Willi tells you that de-activation will bring the Grom back very quickly and suggests a rapid exit. Turn to **70**.

224
You see the vast salt lakes ahead. Suddenly you pick up a message. You are ordered to land immediately. You check visuals and see a GromPol craft; it is not as sleek as usual, but looks like a Mark IV with bits stuck on to it. Do you decide to land (turn to **367**) or fight (turn to **143**)?

225
Turn to **23**.

226
You are tired, battered and now robbed of all your possessions. The Lurgan has flown off, leaving you trussed up. You cannot escape in time to salvage your mission. You have failed.

227

The remaining Bandits give up and speed off. You look around you: the bus is a mess, both the Androids are self-destructing. You move to the pilot's cabin and find the control on 'auto' and a strong whiff of acid on wires. The pilot Android has suffered the same fate. The bus lurches and you jump into the pilot's seat. Auto-control is intermittent. The screen flashes 'Unauthorized User' in bright red letters. You ignore this, while struggling to bring the bus under control. The auto-pilot will not stay on, so you resort to the old saying, 'If all else fails, kick it!' You aim a good kick at the panel, hoping your luck is in. *Test your Luck*. If you are Lucky, turn to **308**; if you are Unlucky, turn to **252**.

228

You feed your credit at the door and press two gravity hours. The door slides open and a flashing light directs you to 'EATS'. Another credit is used to order cube taste ZX 017, one of your favourites and quite a surprise to find on Earth. You climb into your unit, eat the cube and wash it down with some Mangola. You shut the unit and a gas hisses in to send you to sleep for the paid-up time. Deduct 2 TIME units. Add 6 STAMINA points. You wake up feeling refreshed, get out and carry on along the road. Turn to **83**.

229

Throw three dice and add up the total: this is the distance up. Throw one die and add the number to your STAMINA score: this is your jump. If your jump is equal to or greater than the distance, you have been successful (turn to 32). If you fail, deduct 1 from your STAMINA score and try again. If you cannot get up there, you decide to take the other branch (turn to 372).

230

You walk outside and stare into the distance. There is nothing to be seen. You realize that your only chance of getting food is the dispenser. As you turn around, a solid metal door slams shut and an electronic voice thanks you for your custom and tells you to have a nice day! Deduct 1 STAMINA point. Deduct 2 TIME units and turn to 291.

231

The kid is very fast, but no match for you. You grab hold of him just as he is about to disappear into a windowless building. You turn him around and he lets go of your credit cards. Deduct 1 STAMINA point and turn to 345.

232

'Criminals and Groms, that's all we have on Earth these days. Always glad to see a Rogue Tracer.' The man is the owner of the diner and proclaims himself 'the last of the native independents'. He loves to talk and eventually gets on to the subject of Groms: 'We are second-class citizens on our own planet, although most natives have left for Alphacent: no real jobs here, you see.' He tells you of the Houlgans, whom he describes as 'good boys really'. His son is a member of a gang in Madrid; he is called Jose 90. Add 1 LUCK point. Eventually the bus signals take-off and you rush to board it. As you settle, you realize that you haven't eaten anything. The Grom in front of you is being served a Galterian omelette by his Android. Reduce your STAMINA by 1 point and turn to 22.

233

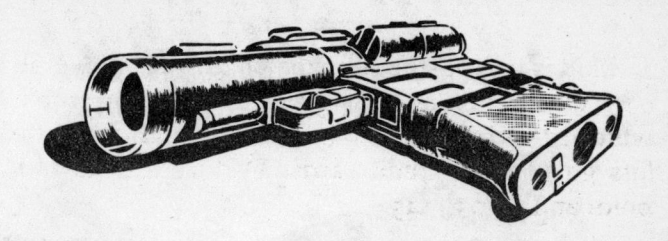

You pick the correct circuit. While you are replacing several leads, you find two wires leading to self-destruct, and you realize that this Android is a walking bomb. The Android recovers and tells you that it will be missed; speed is essential. It will take you to the nearest Grom house with a ComTerm and hold off any attack for as long as necessary. Turn to **43**.

234

You see a road ahead and follow it until a large, flashing star symbol appears. You have no retro fuel so you set down and skid along the road. The Mark III spins to a halt a few metres from a fuel pump. Add 2 LUCK points. A stony-faced Android comes out and asks if you want to 'fill her up'. Turn to **279**.

THE SILVERHOUND Rocket Company

ROUTE MAP

LONDON	0600·1200	MADRID	1030·1630
PARIS	0650·1250	ROMA	1150·1750
ROMA	0810·1410	PARIS	1310·1910
MADRID	0930·1530	LONDON	1430·2030

SH

235

You find that there is only one route that links the northern sector. Most services have been cancelled due to lack of demand and there are considerable delays between stops. While you are working out the times, an Android stands next to you and you feel the CodeMatch pulse on your Chronograph. Deduct 2 TIME units. Do you signal back (turn to **350**) or decide to follow it first (turn to **152**)?

236

The Android drops the jar and it smashes. You're impressed by the use of real glass.

BUTLER
  ANDROID   SKILL 6   STAMINA 6

If you win, the butler self-destructs, leaving a sticky patch on the floor. Turn to **364**.

237

The Grom has top-level security-rating. You ask where the Galactic President is being kept. You get:

Q867   RT88   20KK   169A   824B

The first three sets you know as standard Earth codes for the London area. The last two sets you note down, or note down again in confirmation, if you already have one of them. You rush outside straight into a GromPol Android escorting the real PowerTech. Before it can pull out a stun gun, you are on to it.

GROMPOL ESCORT   SKILL 9   STAMINA 8

If you win, turn to **309**.

238

The Android walks at a standard pace in a westerly direction. Most of the tall buildings are crumbling and, as you walk along, you notice that some side-streets are still inhabited by natives. The Android reaches an area full of bushes and trees from which rises a very old and grand building in an excellent state of repair. Do you attack the Android (turn to **63**) or carry on following it (turn to **135**)?

239

The transport is of standard Galactic General Rocket Motors design and you are skilled in stowing away on these. The robo-loader ignores you as you slip between the plasti-crates and raise the lid of the 'Emergency Humanoid Operators Cab'. You slip in, check the rations and find a good selection. You set your alarm and fall asleep. Add 6 STAMINA points and turn to **208**.

240

When you tip back the seat a pack falls open and you see that it is full of Lurgan speciality food cubes, some of them inside the 'best before' date – a rare treat! Add 2 STAMINA points and turn to **41**.

241

You catch on to the edge of a tallish building and hold on until the fuel in the retro runs out. You unstrap the rocket and let it drop. The Androids below begin to fire at you with their blasters, so you get on to the roof and decide to leap over to the next building. Roll two dice and add up the result: this is the distance to jump. Roll one die and add the number to your STAMINA score: this is your jump. If the jump is equal to or greater than the distance, then you have jumped successfully and can make your way down the stairs to the neighbouring street (turn to **59**). If you fail, you fall.

242

You approach the screen. It is showing a Grom security message about the kidnap of the President. While you stare at the coordinates, an Excel locks its arm round your throat. This is the end of your mission.

243

Your search in the city will be fruitless. The Groms have forbidden all private travel and the next bus out will also be cancelled. Deduct all remaining TIME units. Your mission is over.

244

Deduct 2 TIME units. You dash under cover and dive to the left, then roll away and begin to crawl silently and fast on all fours in approved Rogue Tracer style. The GromPol fires the fore-cannons of the craft. *Test your Luck*. If you are Lucky, the shots miss (turn to **347**). If you are Unlucky, you will have a simple burial in an unmarked grave.

245

The transport is a type you have not seen before, probably of local design. You slip easily between the plasti-crates, but you cannot find an 'Emergency Humanoid Operators Cab'. You sit down and wrap your coat around you and try to get some sleep. Turn to **208**.

246

You leave the shop and head north. The plans are imprinted in your trained mind and you find the hacienda easily. You take your time and find a service entrance with no gates or Guards. You carefully look at the building. Turn to **167**.

247

He says, 'I thought so,' and gas starts to seep into your section of the cockpit. Through a smoky haze, you realize that he is attacking the Silverhound with a group of other craft. Turn to **386**.

248

Lopsti tells the gang to drag you out. They throw you on to the ground and begin to squabble over who should take you on. They eventually decide on some sort of order. You will have to fight each in turn.

	SKILL	STAMINA
First THUG	6	8
Second THUG	7	10
Third THUG	8	8

If you manage to beat the first three gang members, turn to **107**. If you lose, turn to **95**.

Gary Mayes

249

You wake up in a dark, damp, dismal room. You are chained up. You look up and see a hideous sight. A Grom stands before you with snakes growing out of his head. All the time you hear a command inside your brain, 'You will tell us about your mission, you will tell us about your mission . . .' *Test your Fear Factor*. If you are frightened, reduce your STAMINA by 2 points. Repeat the test twice more: if you lose 6 STAMINA points, your control has broken and you have revealed your mission (turn to 57). If you have lost 4 STAMINA points or less, turn to 47.

250

The blaster, set at maximum power, takes the Excel's head off. It staggers, falls and self-destructs. But then the Guard is upon you.

GUARD   SKILL 9   STAMINA 10

If you win, turn to 34.

251

The shop is packed with old pieces of firmware and even has some documents in book format. A pre-Grom technology robot sits at the credit unit and in limited speech asks if it can help. You reply that you are just looking. You sift through various bits and pieces. *Test your Luck*. If you are Lucky, turn to 177. If you are Unlucky, turn to 396.

252

The auto-pilot fails completely. The bus lurches towards the mountains. You take over control again, knowing that you'll have to fly manually all the way. You cannot relax. Reduce your STAMINA by 2 points. Turn to **76**.

253

You notice alarm lights flashing as you travel along. In front of you two heavy metal doors are slowly sliding shut. You think that you might just make it. *Test your Luck*. If you are Lucky, turn to **85**. If you are Unlucky, you are crushed between the doors.

254

You take cover; the police craft circles around. Eventually, they give up the search and fly off. You set off along a road. Turn to **327**.

255

You look carefully at the shaft. There are bars going all the way down, but the spaces between them are greater than your height plus outstretched arms. To descend you must drop and catch each bar in turn. Roll three dice and add up the result: this is the first drop. Roll one die and add the number to your STAMINA score: this is your ability to catch the bar. If your ability is equal to or greater than the drop, then you have successfully caught the first bar. Repeat the procedure two more times. If you ever miss, you fall to your death. If you get down, reduce your STAMINA by 1 point and turn to **389**.

256

While you walk along the road, no craft passes you and you notice that you are heading down towards a river. By the river is a house, very modern in style and by the house is a power launch. You suspect that this is a Grom residence. Do you approach the house (turn to **109**) or give it a wide berth (turn to **60**)?

257

The Android sets off at a fast pace and leads you to a small building, with two GromPols standing at the gate. It tells you that there is a ComTerm inside that can tap into security information, but that it is vacuum-protected and can be accessed only by Androids. The Android will go in, but you will have to keep guard. It unwraps its parcel and hands you a blaster; then it pulls out its own stun gun and rushes into the building. You follow and destroy the first guard with one shot, while the Android punches a hole in the second guard's middle. You take up a defensive position and wait. Turn to **369**.

258

The Grom craft passes over you just as you reach the ZipCar. The rockets fire at once and you speed off with the Grom behind you in close pursuit. A blast from his cannon smashes into your exhaust. You look around the cockpit: you see a button with the word 'Thruster' scrawled above it. This is an illegal item on planet-level craft, but is often used by criminals for getting away. A Thruster will use up all your fuel and you don't even know that it will work. Another shot smashes into your craft. Deduct 2 TIME units. Do you risk pressing the button (turn to 89) or not (turn to 113)?

259

The Android announces, 'Information not available. Groms will be using one of four bases: Madrid, Roma, Paris, London. No other details.' Deduct 2 TIME units and turn to 31.

260

You push open the door and, just as you shut it, you hear the sound of footsteps go past. You look in front of you and there are two other doors with a small terminal to the side of each one. Each door asks for a pass-code and shows the symbol of a knight from a chess set. You must act quickly. Do you choose the left door (turn to 5) or the right door (turn to 112)?

261

The gory scene has made you feel ill. What do you do next? Do you walk away and continue on foot (turn to **379**) or wade into the mess (turn to **9**)?

262

You run fast, keeping close to the buildings and occasionally weaving to avoid stun shots. Suddenly an arm grabs you, and you are halted in your tracks by another group. When they rob you, they come across your ID. This stops them and they take you back to the others. When you find that they detest the Groms, their creators, you explain your mission. They return your possessions and one of them, a recent defector, tells you that it saw the presidential craft brought down near the salt-mines. You have a choice: the Androids will help you get to the salt-mines (turn to **108**), or they will let you continue on your own (turn to **59**).

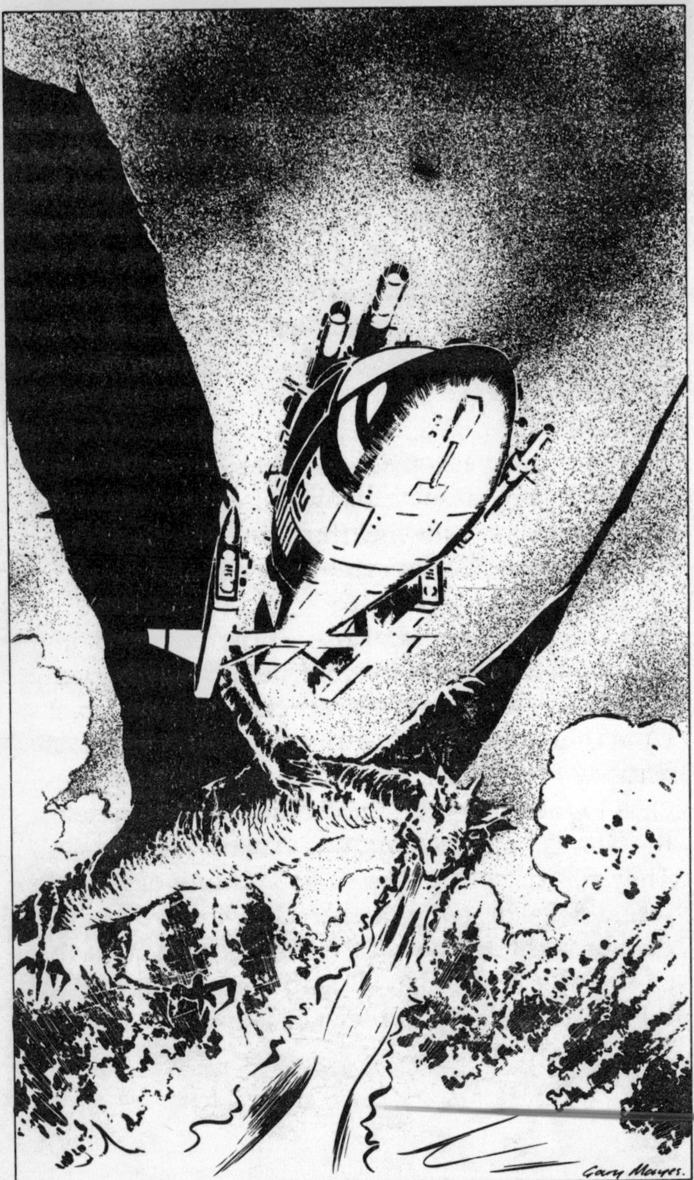
Gary Mayes.

263

You reach the top and stand at the highest point. The Chronograph is now emitting a visual signal. You see the rescue craft coming at Catchnet height and you brace yourself. You are both caught in the plasti-net. You are pulled in and greeted by a spacecruiser commander. The President is taken to his security quarters. You are left standing around. Suddenly the first-lieutenant whistles in amazement, 'What in the galaxy is that?' You look at the Vidscreen: a winged, fire-breathing creature with huge talons is chasing you. The lieutenant waits for your advice. You reply that it's just another Grom illusion. Will you advise him to ignore it (turn to 346) or to fire a missile at it straight away (turn to 155)?

264

You are unwise to run. Before you have taken your second step, it blasts you between the shoulders. It is an Android whose 'cover' has been blown and which is therefore very dangerous. You will recover, but not in time to complete your mission. Deduct all your remaining TIME units.

265

You dig down and cover yourself with the undergrowth. Breathing in the correct way to avoid sense-detect, you try to drop your body temperature in true Rogue Tracer fashion. But when you look ahead, you see a molten flow of lava moving towards you and destroying everything in its path. *Test your Fear Factor*. If you are frightened, your heartbeat speeds up and you are detected: the Excels blast you to smithereens. If you are not frightened, you let the lava flow over you, proving that it is just another illusion. When you think that the coast is clear, you rush across the road. Turn to **213**.

266

You jump on the speedboard and coast along the tunnel in a north-westerly and then northerly direction. Turn to **253**.

267
Test your Luck. If you are Lucky, turn to **21**. If you are Unlucky, turn to **35**.

268
As you wander along, you find the woods getting thicker and darker. You lose all sense of direction. You will never get out of this maze in time to do any good. Deduct all your TIME units. Your mission is over.

269
The Silverhound is hit many times. One of the Androids has lost an arm. You rush around looking for retro-chutes, but you are too late. There is a crash and the bus buries its nose in the soft snow. You lose consciousness as the Androids self-destruct. Turn to **386**.

270

You sit back and watch the flashing lights and controls. After a time you fall asleep. When you wake up, you look out of the window and see the Grom heading back to the craft. Add 1 STAMINA point and turn to **91**.

271

You follow him into the doorway. It is very dark. You hear something clang shut and come across a rusty metal trapdoor, obviously locked from the inside. There is no way to follow him. You go out and stand in the maze of alleyways and buildings. Deduct 2 TIME units and turn to **207**.

272

You are in Black room, Level 4. Reduce OXYGEN by 1 unit. There is one door leading up. Turn to **196**.

273

You think that the hacienda will have a ComTerm which could provide information about the location of the President. What you don't need is a 'rogue' companion interfering in your search. He takes you to the hacienda and then you realize that he intends to leave you there: he is taking no risks. He tells you to take anything valuable, even food. You set off and look through an open gate. Deduct 2 TIME units and turn to **167**.

274

You leap on to the board, touch a few pressure pads and glide off almost silently. As you speed away, a horned creature bursts out from behind the crates and shrieks at you. The board is light and easy to control but you are not sure about fuel levels. Do you travel flat out (turn to **253**) or at half speed to conserve fuel (turn to **148**)?

275

You stand up and walk over to Orvium, pushing his guards aside; you tell him that you want to talk. He is drunk and refuses to talk to anyone who hasn't played 'the game'. He sits you down opposite one of his gang and throws an old six-chamber stun gun down on to the table. He puts a charge in one chamber and then spins it. Your opponent picks up the gun and puts it to his head. Roll one die: that is the chamber. Roll the second die: that is his go. If the numbers match, he has blown his brains out. Now it is your turn: roll the second die again. Take alternate turns until one of you is dead. If you survive, deduct 2 TIME units and turn to **165**.

276

You pull out your Catchman and fire at one of the Houlgans; you punch a second and the rest run away. The Android picks up its boxes and thanks you in what is quite an emotional voice. You signal CodeMatch and, when it realizes who you are, it drops its boxes again! When it has calmed down it introduces itself as a WIL-1 Android, so you decide to call it Willi. It tells you that the President is almost certainly not in Madrid, but in one of the other cities. There should be information about his location at the Plaza de Toros base station. The Groms are great organizers and everything is filed. The Plaza de Toros building is accessible only to Androids and is heavily guarded by many troops of Excels. Turn to **380**.

277

Before you know anything, it has blasted you. You are paralysed and collapse in a heap. Your mission is over.

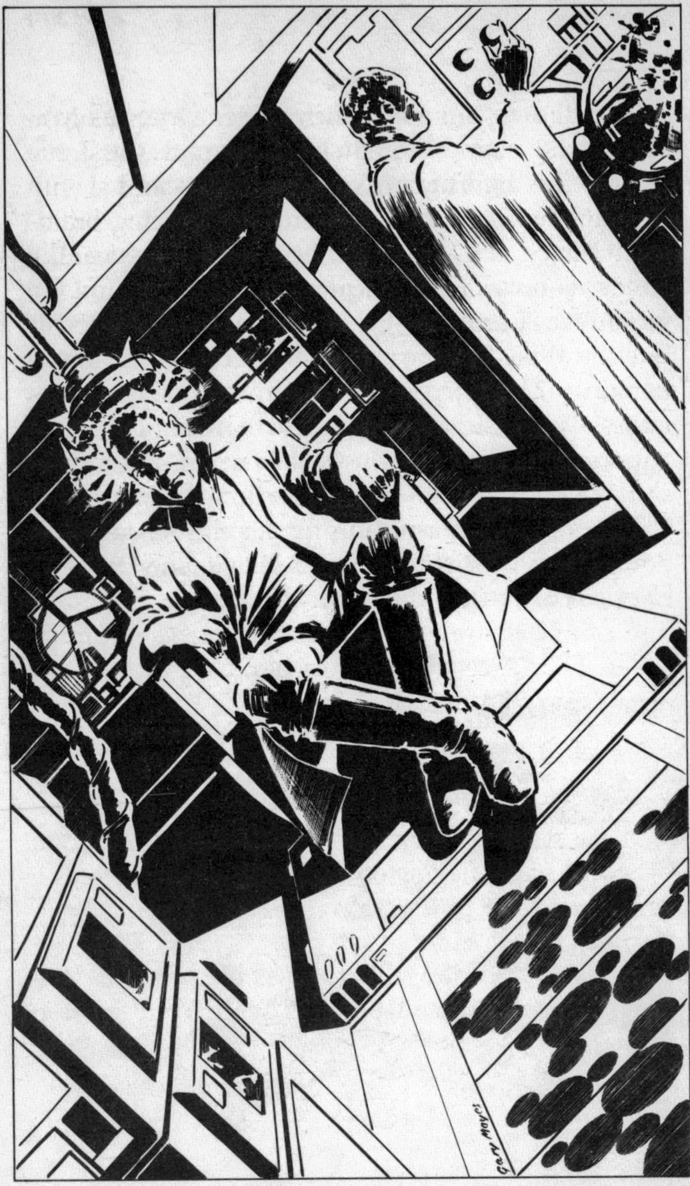
Gary Mayes

278

You come to a door which slides open as you approach... and there in front of you is the President! There are no guards, just a Grom scientist with his back to you. The President is still being brain-scanned, so you know that he has yet to reveal the codes. You wrench the scanner off his head and the Grom turns around. He nearly faints with fright, but then he disappears from your sight, using a personal Illus-o-Scope. You grab the President; he is unresponsive, so you have to carry him out. Reduce your STAMINA by 4 points. The Chronograph shows you that there is a tall structure fairly close; you'll need to get on top of it for the rescue. The door you came through is now sealed, so you check the panels around the room for another exit. You find one that sounds hollow and you kick it in. It collapses and leads into a very old, dark tunnel, full of 200-year-old rubbish. Turn to **24**.

279

You pick up some food cubes and a Mangola tube. Add 4 STAMINA points. While you crunch your 'wheaty snaps' flavoured cube you set a course for Paris (turn to **78**) or London (turn to **217**).

280

The Mark I handles well and after a while you see the city: an overgrown mass of crumbling buildings. Madrid control gives you settings for the Silverhound terminal and you perform a good landing on manual drive. You park in the craft-park. Turn to **179**.

281

Self-destruct begins at its feet as it dutifully answers your question, 'The administrative building is for Androids only: even Groms cannot get physical access, but make contact through their ComTerms. You can get . . .' Before it can give you any further information, its speech functions disintegrate and the rest of the Android dissolves into the ground. Deduct 2 TIME units and turn to **31**.

282

You are correct: $(A - C) \div 2 = B$. A sub-menu appears and asks for a question. You key in: 'Is the Galactic President in Madrid?' It answers in the negative. Then you ask it where the President is being kept. It replies, 'He is at a high-security Base station,' and a symbol appears of a circle with a horizontal line through it. The message continues, 'Reference 169A . . .', but it breaks off and another message asks for your Grom family code letter. Then 'ILLEGAL ACCESS' begins to flash across the screen. You rush back to the exit. Deduct 2 TIME units and turn to **194**.

283

You stand outside the base station on a long straight road, which runs from east to west. You have no local map of the area, since you expected to find one at the station, but none were available. Will you go east (turn to **327**) or west (turn to **103**)?

284

You are in Turquoise room, Level 4. Reduce OXYGEN by 1 unit. There is a door leading up. Turn to **144**.

285

Arana has given you good directions. You see a Vidnews machine, and you insert a credit and scan the files: the news of the kidnap is still being suppressed. Next to the machine stands an old man selling a strange cold food, on a cone. You watch as a native buys one and walks away licking the substance. You have been warned of the hazards of open food, but you give in to the temptation. As you walk along licking in the approved manner, you come across a roadblock, manned by a GromPol task-force. You show one of the Androids your ID and it grabs you. Do you fight (turn to **358**) or go peacefully (turn to **218**)?

286

You head for the Plaza de Toros. Jose explains that it is built under a Grom Ents Complex. The Groms have revived bullfighting and have built their own bulls, since the real ones died out many years ago. The gang take you to a manhole they sometimes use to get in to see some of the Grom sports. As you turn a corner you bump into a wanted criminal, fairly high on the list. Do you attack as a Rogue Tracer (turn to **74**) or ignore him (turn to **114**)?

287

You know that Houlgans are famed for their skill in stealing, so you do not show them any credits but merely hint at the prospect of payment. They are suspicious and begin to back away muttering about Grom agents. How do you win them over? If you think you know the leader's name, count up the letters of his first name, multiply this number by his tattooed number, and go to that reference. Otherwise, turn to 174.

288

Deduct 2 TIME units. *Test your Luck*. If you are Lucky, turn to 332. If you are Unlucky, turn to 325.

289

You run towards the end of the tunnel, splashing through puddles and tripping in the loose wiring. Suddenly you feel empty space beneath you and you fall down a shaft. *Test your Luck*. If you are Lucky, you catch hold of a hot pipe and slide painfully to the bottom (turn to 351). If you are Unlucky, you fall to the ground with a sickening thud.

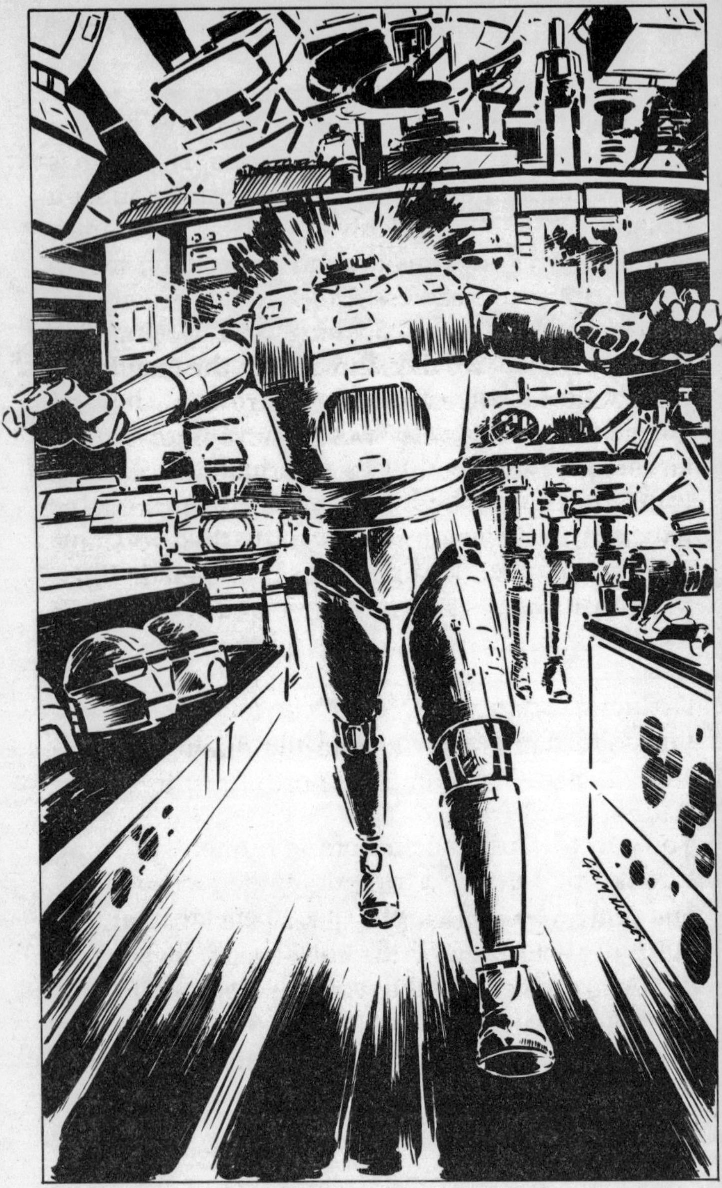

290

You walk in and see a group of assembly Robots putting together a new range of Excels. The room is stacked full of Android parts. In the corner you see a flashing red light. Suddenly a headless Excel grabs you and locks its arms around your body; meanwhile, another headless Excel comes slowly towards you, its arms opening and closing like pincers. Throw two dice and add up the result: this is the Android's strength factor. Throw one die, add the result to your STAMINA score and enter it in the PHYSICAL TASKS box on the *Adventure Sheet*: this is your effort to get free. If your effort is equal to or greater than the Android's strength, then you have broken loose (turn to 348). If it is not, then deduct 1 point from your STAMINA score and try again. If you do not break free, you are finished.

291

You walk along a track from the diner until you reach a road. Will you head north (turn to 363) or south (turn to 256)?

292

The Catchman works. You aim at the legs, but the plasti-net is torn up by the bull straight away. You decide to dodge away, but you leave it very late, and the bull is almost upon you. *Test your Luck*. If you are Lucky, the horns have missed you and you run left to a shelter (turn to 111). If you are Unlucky, farewell, brave matador!

293

You sit down with the gang and order a Mangola, but Orvium insists that you drink a Boolean Snapspine cocktail. When it arrives, you happen to notice, in the corner of the bar, Brak 9 and two grubby Excels, which have obviously been pirated from the Groms. He knows you very well, so you sit lower in your chair and order another Snapspine. By the time Brak has left you have had ten drinks and you are very drunk. Lose 4 STAMINA points and 1 SKILL point. You wave goodbye to the gang and weave your way through the back-streets. Suddenly you fall into something and everything goes blank. Turn to 313.

294

You bank left and start climbing over the mountains. As you gain height you realize that Rocket Bikes are meant only for low-level flying and are not equipped for altitude. You look for somewhere to land with some cover, but there is nowhere. You push the bike to its limit and try to make it over the nearest hill. The rocket stalls and you crash lethally into a rocky outcrop.

295

It's very dark in the corridor. There is a curtain at the end, and you can hear music. You pull it aside and you see a 3-D Vid of a very old film that you once saw on channel 44: 'Starblasters'. You hear a man's laugh in the circular auditorium. He asks you what you want. You reply, 'Orvium.' He gets up; he is huge and carries four blasters strapped to various parts of his body. He asks you your business and you mention the Grom firmware. He looks you up and down and says he'll take you to Orvium. Turn to **176**.

296

You stay where you are and pretend to ignore the images. Then a Grom appears in front of you. He tells you that psychologically you should have shown some interest and that they suspect you of a rescue attempt. Their galactic 'moles' have told them that a Rogue Tracer is on such a mission. All they want is an admission that you are that Rogue Tracer. Deduct 2 TIME units. Do you admit to the accusation (turn to **57**) or keep silent (turn to **122**)?

297

You press 'B' and you briefly see '169A' . . . and then the screen goes blank. You make a mental note of this code (if you do not already have it). Turn to **368**.

298

You call out and she stops and turns around. You remember where you saw her before: at a 'kill' on Bollitrin 444. She is Arana, a very good Rogue Tracer. There is an immediate bond between you and you share information. She tells you that the Groms have hired her for a 'special'. Orvium Egburg has stolen some unprotected firmware from Records Base in Roma and she suspects that there is some important information on those chips. The Groms got her in yesterday and dropped her at the terminal. Do you offer to help (turn to **349**) or carry on operating on your own (turn to **142**)?

299

You drop your cubes and chase after him. When you are outside you see him signalling towards a group of Rocket Bikers in the far corner of the craft-park. You immediately whip out your Catchman and pull the trigger. Throw one die. If you throw 4 or under, your weapon has jammed and you take him on unarmed. If you throw 5 or 6, then Lopsti is caught (turn to **121**).

LOPSTI   SKILL 6   STAMINA 8

If you win, turn to **121**. If you lose, turn to **19**.

300

You follow its advice and go through the door. You are immediately grabbed by three GromPol Androids. Deduct 2 TIME units and turn to **322**.

301

You look carefully at the edges of the door for light beams or wiring. Suddenly, an Android arm grabs you from behind in a strong grip. You give way and collapse out of its grip. You realize that you'll have to fight it quickly and silently.

GUARD   SKILL 9   STAMINA 8

If you win, the Android self-destructs. Turn to **260**.

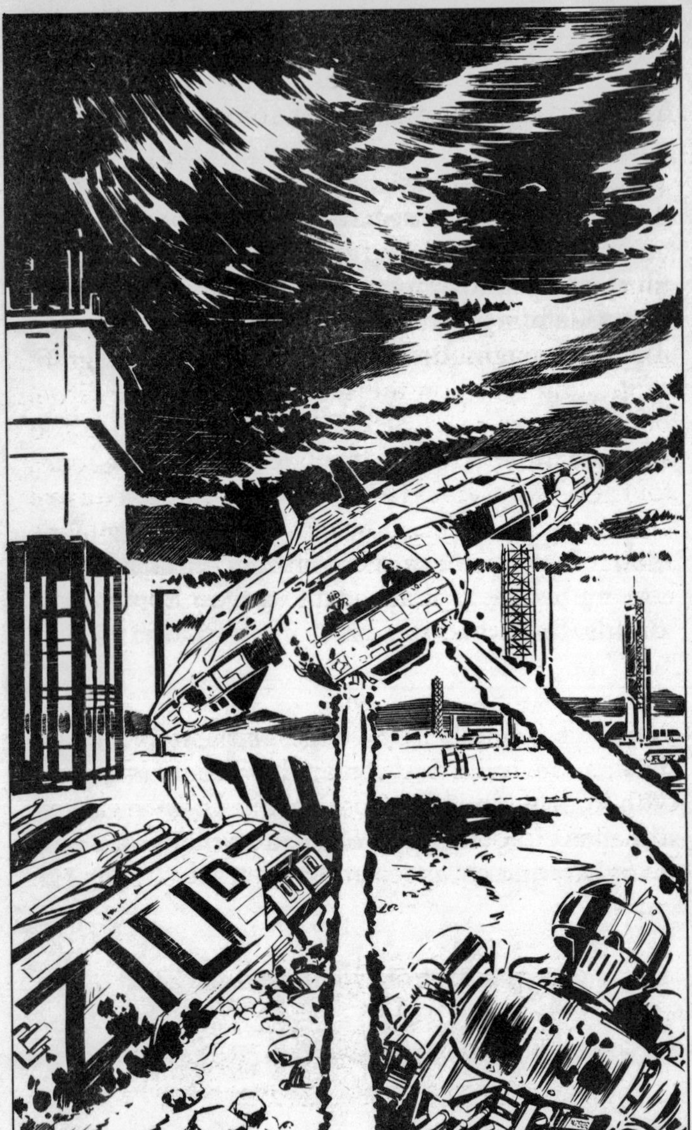

302

You land close to the site of some debris from a space lifeboat. You walk around and find parts of a shattered presidential Guard Android. Self-destruct circuits must have broken up before they could operate. You find two recall chips and plug them into your Chronograph. You can see the event of the landing through the Guard's vision. You replay the episode with high-intensity magnification and focus on the setting used by the Grom pilot. You can see: Q867 RT88 20KK 169A . . . You know that the first three groups are standard codes for the London area. Then you look up and see a real Grom craft heading towards you with cannons firing. The shots destroy the head of the Guard. You can run for the ZipCar (turn to 258) or for a nearby salt trench (turn to 3).

303

The wolf is snarled up in the plasti-net. You run back for the fence, but you are headed off by a pack of them that appear in front of you. They chase you into a building and up an old staircase that suddenly gives way and collapses under you. Turn to 313.

304

Before you can say anything, the Android shouts that you are under arrest. It pulls out its stun gun and you run off round the corner. When it follows you are waiting for it.

ANDROID   SKILL 8   STAMINA 8

If you win, turn to **179**.

305

To your left is an abandoned retro pack. You go over and pick it up. There just might be enough fuel left. In a hail of stun shots, you strap it on, ignite the rockets and shoot off in an uncontrollable arc. *Test your Luck*. If you are Lucky, turn to **241**. If you are Unlucky, you have crashed into a building and your mission ends here.

306

You walk over to the bar and talk to the girl. 'It has kept us here since yesterday when it came in and demanded a drink,' she says. 'I gave it some lubricant, but it wanted beer and told me to play this ridiculous instrument.' She holds up a thin box with some wires across it. You guess that the Excel has suffered memory corruption and has its 'data bus pins' crossed. It must believe that it is living in the past. You have a good knowledge of VidEnts and realize that it believes it is in what was known as a 'Western'. Turn to 58.

307

You notice that the elevators work on the balance principle, and so probably require no power. You get the President in, shut the metal grille and turn a large lever. There is a lot of creaking and shuddering, but it begins to work. Turn to 338.

308

The auto-pilot reasserts itself and sets up the flight path to Paris. You sit back, eat some food cubes and get some sleep. Deduct 2 TIME units. Add 6 STAMINA points and turn to **76**.

309

As you make your way through the city you check your Chronograph and realize that you will need transport to London as soon as possible. You see a transport craft marked 'Escargot' and crates labelled with a circle and a horizontal line through it. Do you stow away on the transport (turn to **239**) or go back to the Silverhound terminal (turn to **134**)?

310

The door slides shut behind you. You are in the side-street behind the Plaza de Toros. Your Chronograph beeps at you and you realize that you have to catch the bus. You look over your shoulder as a Guard comes out of the same door, fires a blast in the other direction and runs off. You make your way to the terminal. Add 2 LUCK points and turn to **80**.

311

You drag the GromPol behind a cupboard, but it begins to self-destruct in your hands. You walk towards a door marked 'NO ADMITTANCE – EXCEL CLASS ONLY.' The door slides open easily; there is no one around. In front of you is a ComTerm and on the screen you see:

11	19	29
6	11	16
17	17	?

Key in the missing number and go to that section. You will be told straight away if you are correct. If you cannot work out the missing number, turn to **194**.

312

You give him a likely felon's name. The Grom is immediately suspicious: Rogue Tracers never reveal targets even under pain of brainscan. He lets the bus go. He stares at you and you stare back, noticing how slight he is and how useless he would be in a fight. Just then he disappears and the inside of the craft becomes a square white box. The walls, roof and ceiling begin to close in on you. Spikes appear all over the surfaces and begin to ooze blood. *Test your Fear Factor*. If you are frightened, deduct 2 STAMINA points. Everything blacks out. Turn to **182**.

313

You wake up with a very sore head and look around. You are in a set of crumbling underground catacombs. There is a strong damp smell. You walk along a corridor which goes from one chamber to another. Each chamber has a dome-like ceiling. You then look down at your feet and notice water seeping in from the direction you are walking in. Soon it is up to your knees. You see a light in the distance: could it be a way out? Deduct 2 TIME units and turn to **394**.

314

You plead that you did not know and are told that ignorance of the law is no excuse. Do you fight your way out (turn to **399**) or go quietly (turn to **168**)?

315

You pay and discuss the help you need. You let them know that you want access to a highly placed Grom ComTerm. They argue among themselves, but decide on two likely places: the Plaza de Toros or the hacienda. The former is accessible only to Androids, but they think that they can get you in. The hacienda is less heavily guarded. Do you choose the Plaza de Toros (turn to 286) or the hacienda (turn to 183)?

316

You go up to the screen and look at the information. You know that it is all false and that the screen is just an illusion. The Groms are using a double-bluff technique to see if you pretend to show no interest. You touch nothing and watch the screen. Deduct 2 TIME units and turn to 6.

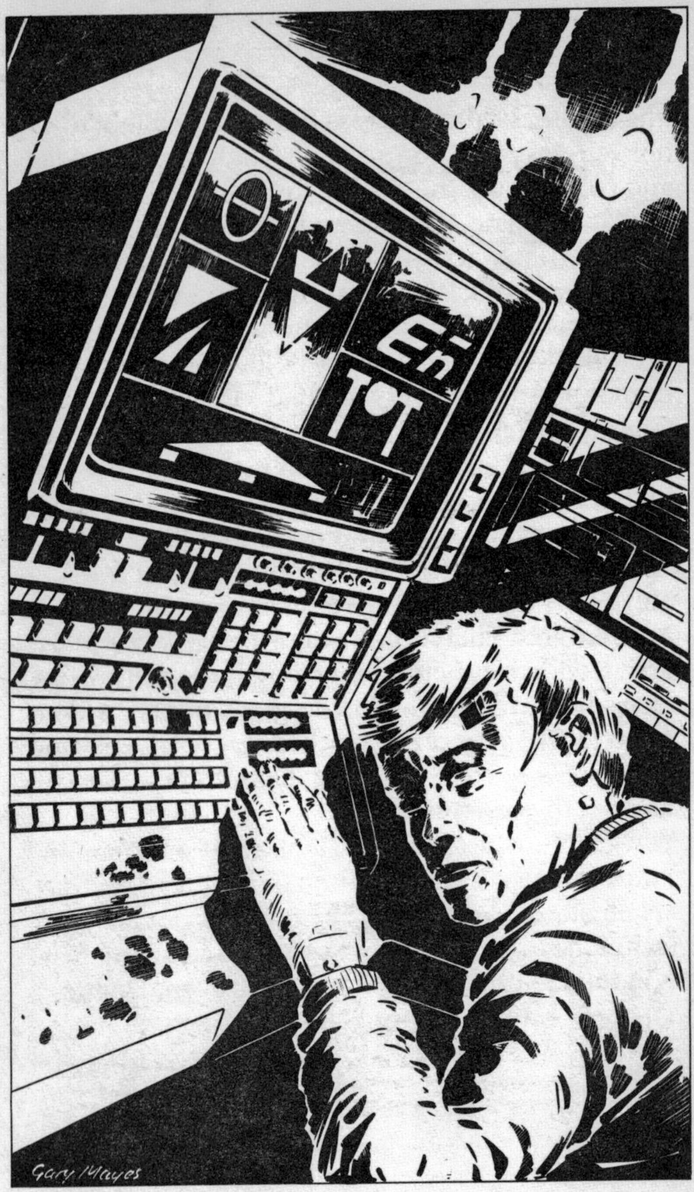
Gary Mayes

317

The Android slumps across the keyboard, but does not self-destruct. You scroll through various codes and come across the one for the Galactic President. You investigate this file and you get a screen of symbols (look at the illustration). The one on the top-left corner flashes; it seems to be some sort of clue. As you begin to delve into sub-menus, you feel the CodeMatch signal from Willi. You go out and find the Android very excited. It tells you that Guards are on their way: they have sensed the loss of the ComTerm Android. Willi suggests that you hide while it takes care of them. Do you agree (turn to 223) or stand and fight (turn to 105)?

318

You are in a chamber. In the corner stands a de-activated Excel. Behind it is a door marked with a chess knight symbol. Do you go through the door (turn to 387)? There is a blocked exit north-east and other exits north (turn to 353), south (turn to 139) and south-west (turn to 62).

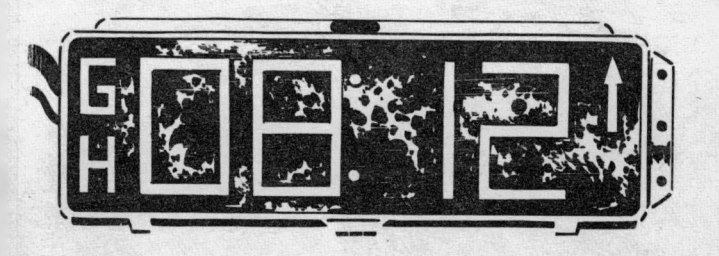

319

You stand back in a doorway and watch carefully. The Houlgans are intent on robbing the Android. They poke at its arms and legs. By now it has dropped all of its boxes and one or two have been picked up by them. They know that a standard service Android has no real fighting prowess. One of them suddenly stabs it in the side. There is a spark and the Android moves with tremendous speed, whips out a stun gun and hits all of them in a few seconds. It knows that you have seen everything and it runs towards you. Do you run (turn to **264**) or raise your hands to show that you will not fight (turn to **128**)?

320

You hack your way through the forest until you are exhausted. You sit down and a Gromasaurus steps on you!

321

You are right to worry about safety, but you are exhausted and should have had a rest when you had the chance. Deduct 2 STAMINA points and turn to **41**.

322

You are thrown into a dark room. You are deprived of all your senses until a Gromulan face appears before you and, in a voice that seems to surround you, tells you that they know about your mission through their galactic 'moles'. All they need is for you to confess and you will not be harmed. Do you confess (turn to **57**) or say nothing (turn to **249**)?

323

You approach carefully, with your back to the crates. Suddenly a strange, horned, dog-faced creature leaps out at you. Its coarse hands grip your throat and fangs lodge in your shoulder.

HORNED DOG-
  FACED GUARD   SKILL 9   STAMINA 8

If you win, turn to **266**.

324

Although you are tired, you force yourself on. Deduct 1 STAMINA point. As you pass a group of Houlgans, one of them brushes against you and takes your Catchman. The others stand around and cheer. You run after him, catch him and take back your property. Deduct another STAMINA point. You are shattered. Do you change your mind about the sleep unit (turn to **228**) or carry on (turn to **83**)?

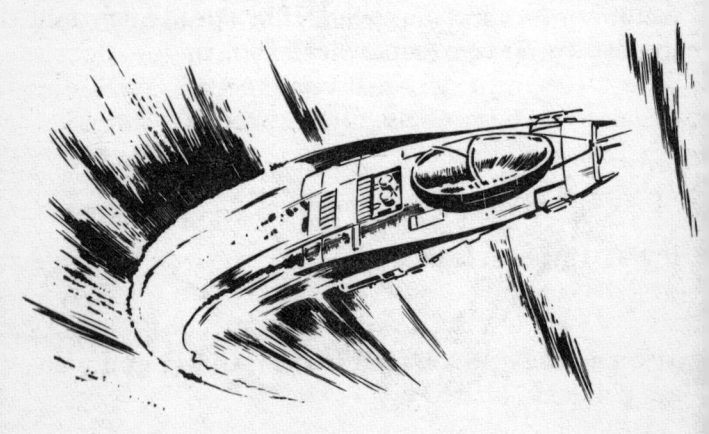

325

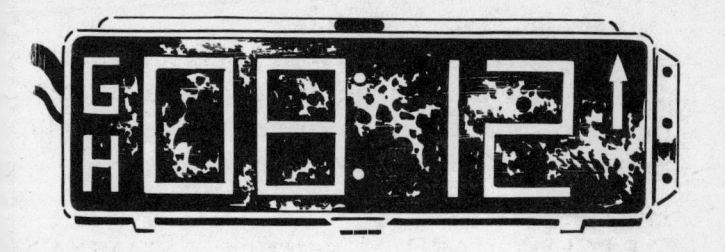

You are being chased by a Horned Dog-Faced Guard. It fires a blaster at you and you weave from side to side. The shots smash into the tunnel walls. Throw one die for your position and throw the second die for the blast. If the blast is the same as your position, then you have been badly hit and take no more interest in the mission. Repeat this procedure three times. If you survive, you try to outrace the Guard.

Throw two dice: this is your speed. Throw two dice again for the Guard's speed. If its speed is greater than yours, it has caught you and you have to fight it with the neutronsword. If your speed is greater or equal, it crashes into the tunnel wall (turn to 332).

HORNED DOG-
 FACED GUARD   SKILL 9   STAMINA 8

If you win, turn to 332.

326

Test your Luck. If you are Lucky, turn to 180. If you are Unlucky, turn to 343.

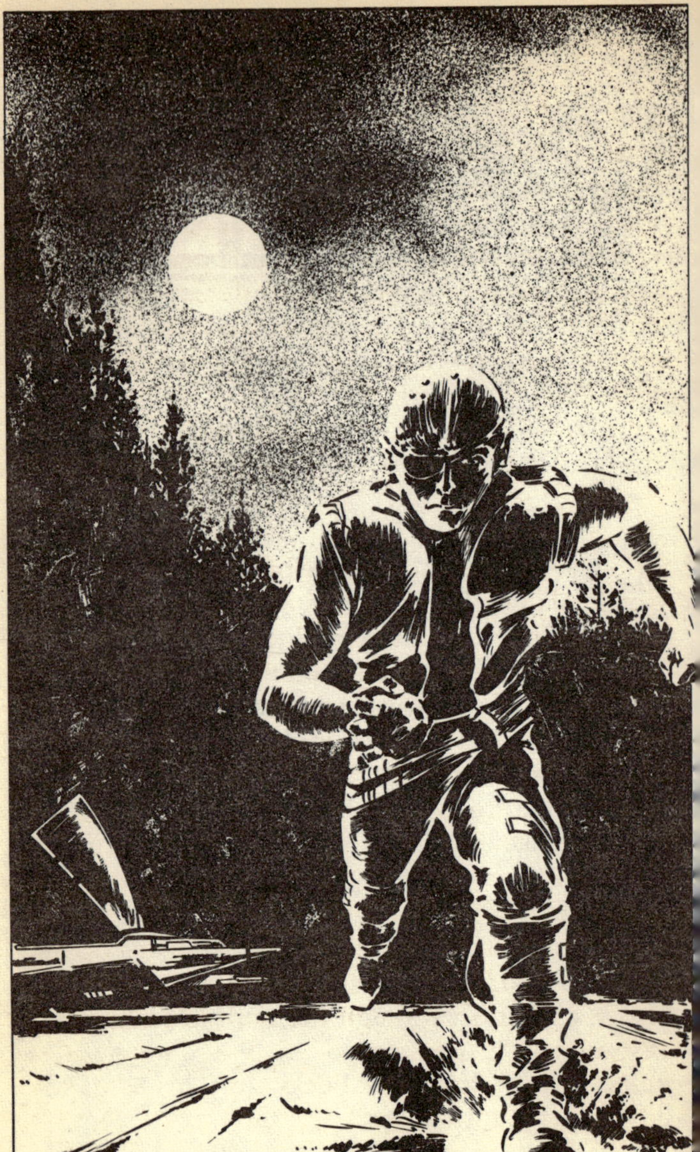

327

You walk for a long time along the road, which is often overgrown. You are getting tired, hungry and thirsty: reduce your STAMINA by 1 point. Just then, you see a battered ZipCar at the side of the road with its hood up. There seems to be no one around, and you approach carefully. Suddenly someone leaps out of the bushes. You spin around just in time to see the Lurgan who is rushing at you hurl a large rock. *Test your Luck*. If you are Lucky, he has missed (turn to 388). If you are Unlucky, you've been hit on the head (turn to 226).

328

While you dash off down the back-streets, you hear a craft taking off very close by and obviously looking for you. In your haste you find yourself in a blind alley. There is an open warehouse door on the right and a pile of rubble on a broken manhole on the ground in front of you. Do you go into the warehouse (turn to 365) or down the manhole (turn to 87)?

329

You climb up. As you get higher, the metal bars get dirtier and full of cobwebs. The shaft leads up into darkness. Suddenly the shaft gives way and you fall down and crash through the floor. You lose consciousness. Turn to 313.

330

Fortunately you land on some soft ground between two boulders. You take cover straight away, because you become aware of other craft up above, which are obviously looking for you. Turn to **137**.

331

Deduct 2 TIME units. You are in a chamber with a blocked tunnel south, and exits west (turn to **48**), east (turn to **27**) and north (turn to **139**).

332

You are in a rubble-strewn chamber. There is a blocked exit to the east, and exits north (turn to **71**) and south (turn to **56**).

333

You wake up by an anti-gravity pool, facing a small Grom who is sipping a long, cool drink. A service Android offers you a glass. The Grom admits that he was bored and arranged the 'entertainments'. He talks for hours and lets slip that he is highly placed in Grom HQ Madrid. When he leaves you for a moment, you notice a ComTerm showing an image of the President. Do you approach the ComTerm (turn to **242**) or stay where you are (turn to **190**)?

334

The door easily slides open. You are in a small, narrow corridor. There are several smudges on the floor and another door at the end of the corridor. On one of the walls is a mirror which you suspect of being two-way. Suddenly the second door opens and you are crushed into a smudge on the floor. Two Grom scientists, who are conducting experiments on extreme high pressure, look through the glass and wonder what caused the extra stain.

335

You shrug your shoulders, turn around and eat your cubes. The man goes away and you sit in silence until the bus signals for take-off. Add 2 STAMINA points and turn to 22.

336

Deduct 2 TIME units. You are in a chamber with exits east (turn to 12), west (turn to 37) and south (turn to 326).

337

'Hello,' says the Android. 'I'm sorry, sir, I have lost all automotive functions and cannot complete my tasks. I will self-destruct now.' You order it to shut up and to tell you the way out of the tunnel. It insists that it must self-destruct, but it seems to have broken the circuits which enable it to do so. You bargain with it that you will help, if it tells you the way out. It thinks for a while; its eyes dim and then light up. 'Okay,' it announces. It tells you to take the tunnel and walk for four hundred metres, then take the left fork and on the third foundation shaft you will find a ladder leading up into the Ents Complex. You connect up its circuits and it begins to dissolve with what could be a smile on its face. You walk to the ladder. Turn to **25**.

338

You come up into a devastated landscape with the faint green tinge of radioactivity. You see the tower a short distance away. The Chronograph emits the coded rescue signal when you reach the bottom of the structure. There is no one around and you suspect that the very high radioactivity is responsible. The tower is just a block of concrete with a ladder on the side. You will need all your strength to climb it with the President on your shoulders. Throw two dice: this is the strength factor needed to get to the top. If this is greater than your STAMINA score, then you collapse halfway up the ladder and both of you fall to your deaths. If you make it to the top, turn to **263**.

339

The Android stutters as its feet begin to dissolve, 'Madrid records at Plaza de Toros . . . west of here . . . Androids only . . .' The decay reaches the speech circuits and the Android is silent. Deduct 2 TIME units and turn to **117**.

340

There are pieces of Android all over the room. The pieces dissolve through the floor and then the floor gives way and you fall through. Turn to **333**.

341

Your fight with Lam causes a commotion. The Excels are upon you and they put you in a holding cell for eighty gravity hours. Deduct all your remaining TIME units. You have no time left to complete your mission.

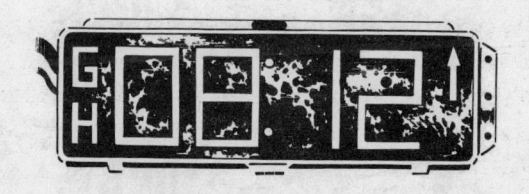

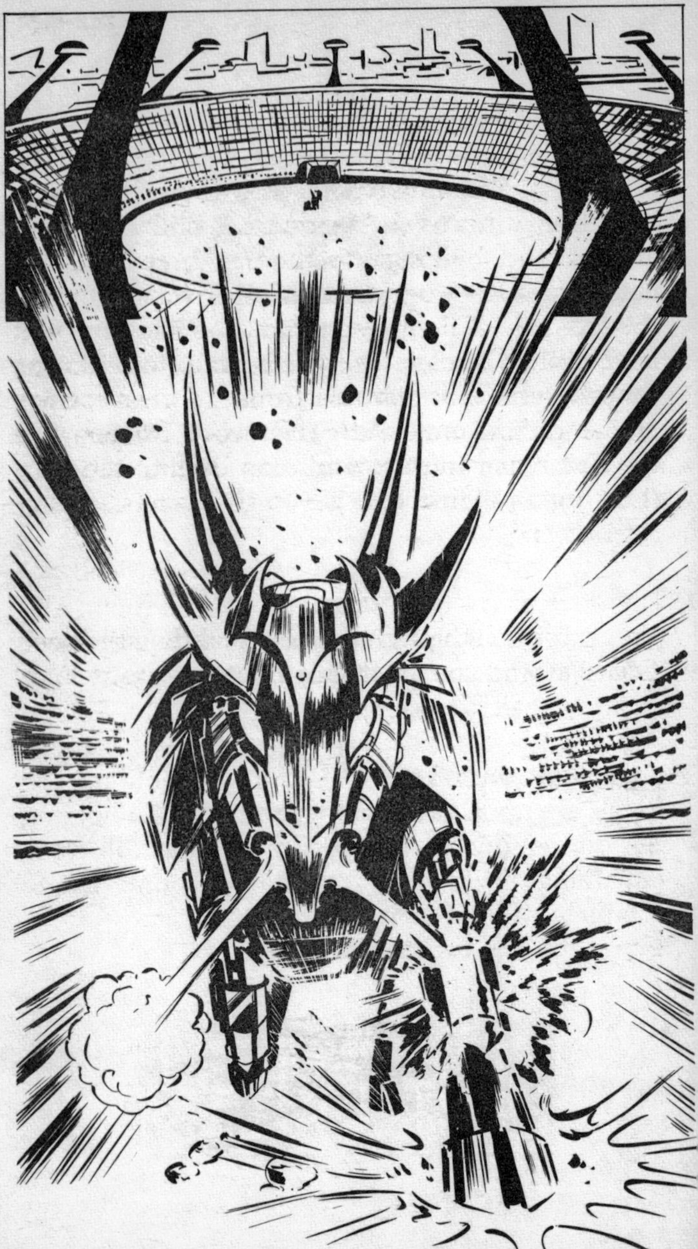

342

You are in a stadium. There is a very high wall all around, and across on the far side is a strange creature of Gromulan make, like a huge bull with long, steely horns. It stands stock-still. You look around the bullring; there are three shelters, equidistant from one another. You walk carefully towards one of them and notice, too late, that you have broken a beam. The bull is activated. It turns towards you, gives an electronic snort, scrabbles at the ground and charges at you. Do you use the Catchman (turn to **292**), run back to the door (turn to **185**), or dodge left to the nearest shelter (turn to **111**)?

343

You run into a squad of four Horned, Dog-Faced Guards, who are clutching neutronswords. You must fight all four in turn.

	SKILL	STAMINA
First GUARD	8	8
Second GUARD	7	8
Third GUARD	9	10
Fourth GUARD	8	10

If you survive, turn to **180**.

344

You climb up a vertical shaft. There is a metal plate at the top which unlocks and swings open. You are in the middle of a Roman street. A ZipCar thunders overhead. You get out and slam the cover shut. The alarm on the Chronograph beeps at you and you realize that the Silverhound for Paris is due to leave soon. Do you go to the terminal (turn to **75**) or stay and carry on your investigation (turn to **221**)?

345

You are faced with a frightened boy who looks as though he hasn't had a good meal in days. You put him at ease and tell him that you want his gang's help. He takes you to a bar where the R'al Houlgans hang out. Turn to **132**.

346

You are unwise to underestimate Grom ingenuity. The Dragon is a mega-missile with built-in Illus-o-Scope and anti-sensor devices. The missile ploughs into the rescue craft, destroying everyone.

347

You run silently and fast through the undergrowth. The craft fires again, but is off target. Four Excels begin to comb the area. You reach the edge of the gardens and there is nothing but open space ahead of you. The Excels are watching the edges, stun guns ready and set on maximum power. Others are using heat-detector units. Do you sit tight (turn to 265) or run for it across the open ground (turn to 213)?

348

Alarms flash as you get out into the loading-bay. There you see a Grom commercial transport, which is about to take off. The plasti-crates are all marked with a circle with a horizontal line through it. Deduct 2 TIME units. Do you wish to stow away on the transport (turn to 245) or go to the Silverhound terminal (turn to 134)?

349

As you walk along she tells you all the details. She suspects Orvium is going to sell to the highest bidder. You tell her your mission, for Rogue Tracers have no secrets from each other, and she has no objection to you using the firmware to gain information before she returns it to the Groms. She knows of a few places where Orvium and his cronies hang out. You split up and you have two options: the Roxyrama (turn to 151) or Gino's Club (turn to 285).

350

You look at the Android and press your CodeMatch button. It walks away from you and sits on a bench. You follow and sit next to it, but it does not speak to you and you get suspicious. When you get up, two Excels grab you and you know that the 'planted' Android has been 'turned'. You are dragged away. Your mission has failed.

351

You land in a puddle, your hands burning. You are in a large chamber with an exit to the left. You look up at the shaft, trip over something and fall head-first into the puddle. You feel around and find the head of a service Android and some other bits. You quickly do some temporary repair work on the eye and brain region and you are greeted with a low rumble which sounds like 'Hallo.' Turn to 337.

352

You are in Magenta room, Level 4. Reduce OXYGEN by 1 unit. There is one door leading up. Turn to 144.

353

Deduct 2 TIME units. The tunnel divides. There are exits east (turn to 37), west (turn to 131) and south (turn to 318). To the north is an exit blocked by a heavy steel door.

354

The bikes have an extremely short range and after half a gravity hour they head off for a large flashing Star sign that indicates a fuel station. The attendant service Android beams a manufactured smile at the gang as they fight over the food cubes. Lopsti and your guard intervene. The Android fills the bike you are on first and you notice that the anti-theft device has not been set. Do you start the Rocket Bike and go (turn to **65**) or wait for a better opportunity (turn to **171**)?

355

The wolf attacks and is joined by a pack of about twenty others. You cannot fight them all off and your Catchman has run out. You collapse under their savage fangs.

356

You head north along several twisting roads. You begin to lose your sense of direction, when someone calls you; there is an open gate to your left. Deduct 2 TIME units. Do you go in (turn to **32**) or carry on (turn to **136**)?

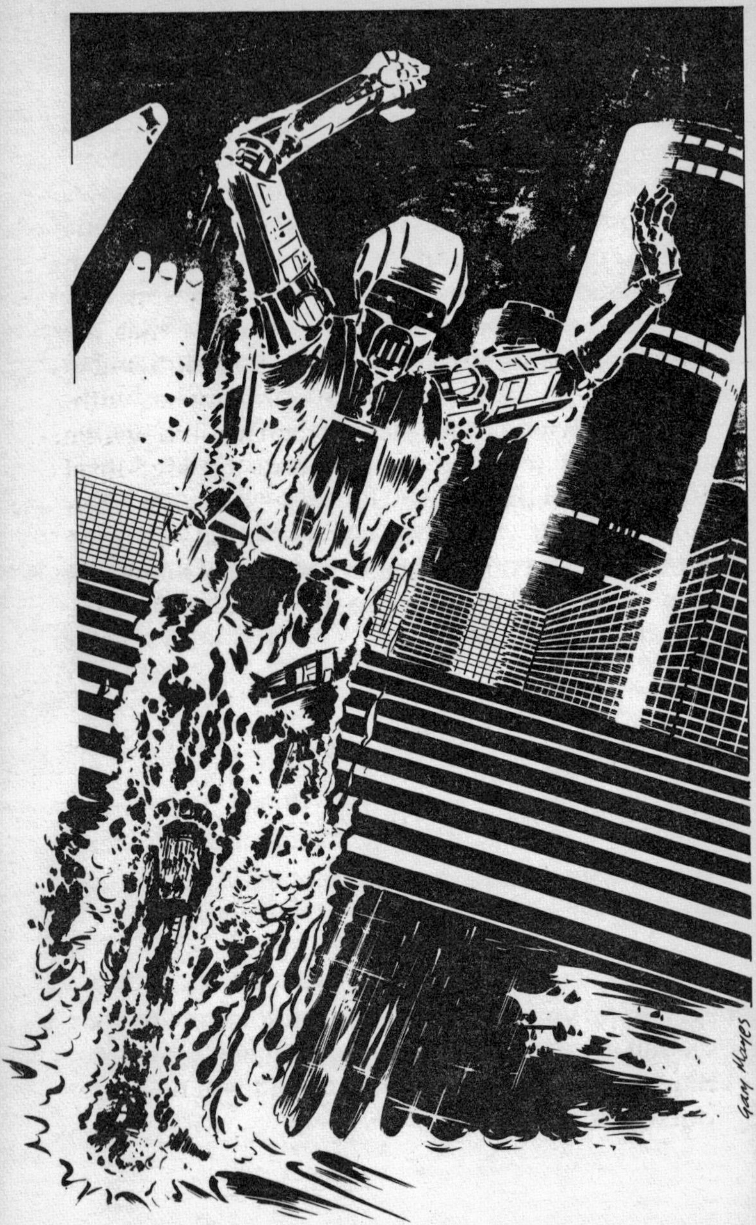
Gary Mayes

357

You walk towards the Android. It drops its vacuum attachment and goes out of a side door. You follow, turn a corner and find it waiting for you. It presses the CodeMatch signal and you respond. It is one of the 'planted' Androids. It gives you as much information as it has gleaned. It tells you that the Groms are based in four cities and that the Silverhound bus is the only mode of public travel to these cities. The Rocket-a-Hire company has withdrawn its services due to lack of demand and private ZipCars are few and far between. All high-level Groms are linked into the bases through their ComTerms. If you can get access to one of these terminals you could probably get a lot of important information. When its message has ended it begins to self-destruct. Turn to **72**.

358

You twist away and then flip over, grabbing the Android by the arms.

GROMPOL ANDROID   SKILL 7   STAMINA 10

If you win, you de-activate the Android, but are surrounded by the task-force. Turn to **218**.

359

As you cut your way through the undergrowth your feet start to feel very heavy and then you cannot move them at all. You are stuck and will never get out of this swamp.

360

Jose asks you how you know his name and you explain about his father's diner. He relaxes, the chains and spears are put away and Jose begins to accept you. He suggests going to get something to eat. Turn to **132**.

361

Deduct 2 TIME units. You walk through the door and it closes behind you. Suddenly a shaft of fire shoots out of the wall, and part of your boot is burnt. Next time you move to avoid the flame, but a section of the floor drops open. Gradually, as the flames continue to shoot out, more and more parts of the floor open up. *Test your Luck*. If you are Unlucky, you have fallen through one of the holes (turn to **201**). If you are Lucky, you are forced into a corner and a sheet of flame envelops your head (turn to **333**).

362

You can hear talking and swearing behind a door. There are two voices. You pull out your Catchman. Do you go in (turn to **93**) or look around some more (turn to **295**)?

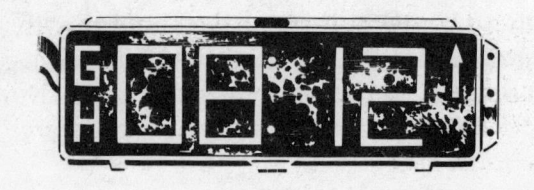

363–364

363

You walk along the road for several gravity hours. Deduct 2 TIME units. Eventually, you reach a small settlement perched on top of a hill. You walk through the town: it is deserted. As you pass the empty buildings you see what must have been the original ZipCar Mark I, rusted and patched, parked outside a building with a flaking sign proclaiming 'Hotel Alcazar'. Do you go into the Alcazar (turn to **197**) or approach the ZipCar (turn to **170**)?

364

You are faced with three doors, but before you can decide which to take, the left door opens and out pops a small Gromulan kid about five gravity years old. She stops, looks you up and down, then asks you what's happened to Beany and her lemonade. You don't reply. She stamps her foot and a knife shoots out of her right eye straight for yours. You instinctively drop to the floor; when you look up a giant boulder falls on top of you. You are not hurt, but you see an image of yourself across the room breaking up, cartoon-style, into little pieces. The little girl laughs. She holds a small Illus-o-Scope in her hand. She asks you to play with her. Do you (turn to **68**), or will you ignore her and search the house (turn to **106**)?

365

You slip into the warehouse as the door slides shut. You look around. It appears to be a Grom Android assembly plant. You are in a room surrounded by immobile, headless Excels. A Forkliftron moves between them. There are two doors ahead. Do you take the left one (turn to **158**) or the right one (turn to **290**)?

366

The Excel demands to know your business. You show it your ID and it disappears. Deduct 2 TIME units. It leaves you standing in a small white box with your head feeling four times its normal size. You know that it's an illusion, but you collapse under its weight. Turn to **201**.

367

You land the ZipCar on a salt lake and get out. The Grom craft approaches, and suddenly fires its cannons at you. *Test your Luck*. If you are Unlucky, you have been hit and you watch helplessly while a couple of Bandits get out of the Grom craft. They strip you of credits and equipment and leave you badly wounded. You cannot complete your mission. If you are Lucky, you escape into a nearby salt trench and the Bandits steal the ZipCar (turn to **3**).

368

Orvium and his cronies come back in and he asks you if that is not the real thing. You agree that it is and you tell him that you have to report back and arrange for credits, but Orvium insists that you stay for a drink. Do you stay (turn to **293**), or get out fast (turn to **186**)?

369

All is quiet. Then suddenly two Androids appear, an Excel and a Guard. You drop just as they fire at you, and they miss. They move fast and you can fire at only one. Do you fire at the Guard (turn to **173**) or the Excel (turn to **250**)?

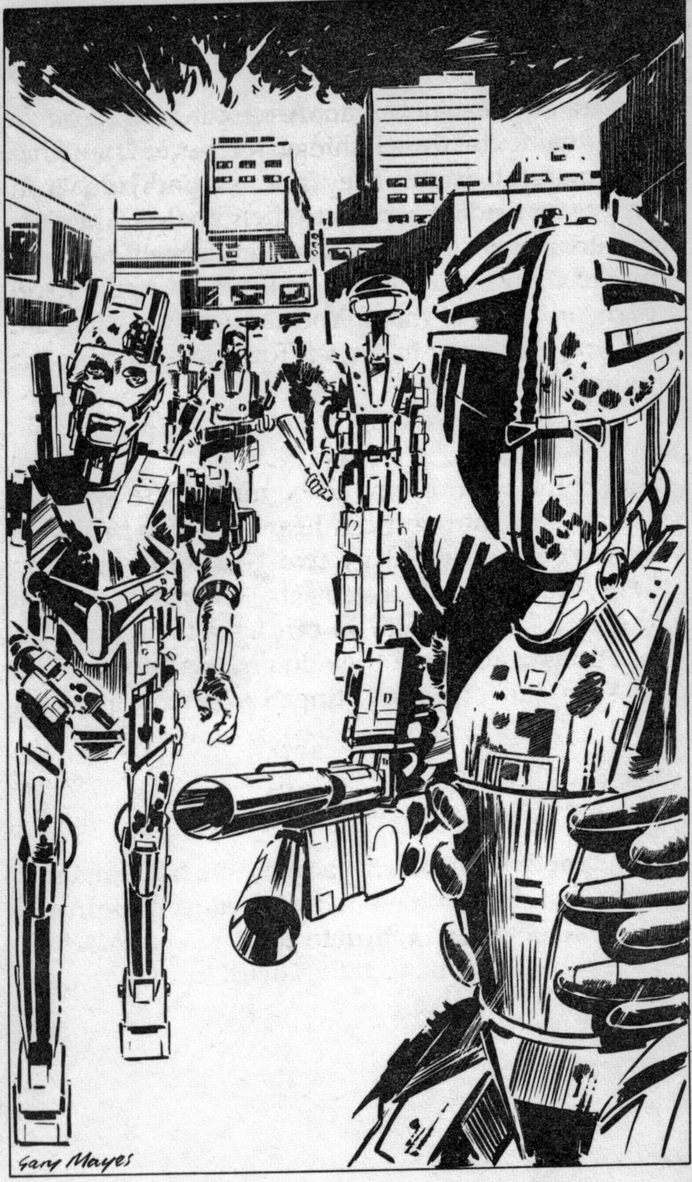
Gary Mayes

370

Ahead of you stands an Android gang. You've heard rumours of such things, but never knew that they really existed. They prey on individuals in order to carry out repairs to their bodies. They are the failures of the early Grom personality experiments. They head towards you and you notice Excel parts on some of them. You cannot fight them all. Do you run away to the left (turn to **262**) or to the right (turn to **42**)?

371

You climb what seems to be an endless spiral of metal steps, but you can hear footsteps following you. You are caught by two Guards in radiation suits, but because the stairs are so narrow you fight them one at a time. You can fight them with the neutronsword, since they do not use stun guns or blasters, but long spikes tipped with neuronsplat.

	SKILL	STAMINA
First GUARD	8	8
Second GUARD	9	10

Remember that you are carrying the Galactic President and should have reduced your STAMINA as directed. If you win, turn to **338**.

372

The tunnel begins to stink and you suspect that the old sewage system is still in use. You look around and suddenly a dark figure leaps on to your back; claws sink into your neck and shoulders. You fall over, forcing the creature to let go, and you see a woman dressed in black with long nails and sharp filed teeth. She snarls and attacks you.

FELINA   SKILL 9   STAMINA 12

If you win, turn to **61**.

373

You join the other shuttle passengers who are feeding their credits into the Visamatic of the Silverhound. After each operation the doors blurt out a distorted 'That'll do nicely.' Turn to **72**.

374

You are surrounded by a mass of huge black rats. You pull out your Catchman as they scramble towards you and set it for wide shooting. Throw two dice: this is the number of rats in the first group. Throw two dice again: this is the number caught by the plasti-net. If any get through, they sink their fangs into your body. Reduce your STAMINA by 1 point for each rat that bites you. Turn to **336**.

375

You find the circuit and it is undamaged. You realize that you cannot save the Android: self-destruct is beginning. Looking carefully at the other circuit, you do not see what you expect. You get up and run. This Android has been fitted with neutron blast in case a walking bomb was needed on the mission. There is a terrific explosion . . .

376

You are still being chased when the tunnel forks. Deduct 2 TIME units. Do you go left (turn to **162**) or right (turn to **73**)?

377

You are in Grey room, Level 4. Reduce OXYGEN by 1 unit. There is one door leading up (turn to **146**) and one door leading out (turn to **310**).

378

You head for the left-hand shelter. The bull charges you and you stand up in front of it with your spears held aloft.

BULL ANDROID   SKILL 7   STAMINA 6

If you lose, you have been badly gored and are unable to continue your mission. If you win, you have damaged the bull, which has now fallen over and is leaking lubricant. You rush to the shelter and find a door. Deduct 2 TIME units and turn to **88**.

379

You get back on the road, shuddering after your nasty experience. You trudge along, but see no sign of any craft. You are tired, hungry and running out of time. Deduct all remaining TIME units. You fail to reach the President.

380

Willi tells you that its master is a low-ranking Grom, whose ComTerm has probably not got full access to the Plaza de Toros base station. Deduct 2 TIME units. Willi leads you towards its master's house. Turn to 36.

381

The GromPol craft accelerates and soon flags down the bus. The GromPol Android tells you to have a nice day. You get on board. The other passengers try to ignore you. Turn to 22.

382

You sit back and watch the power launch skim over the water. An Android brings you a Mangola and you check your Chronograph. Deduct 2 TIME units and add 4 STAMINA points. The trip is fast. You land close to the centre of the city, and an Excel gets off the launch. You see an old flaking sign, 'Estacion del Norte', which you assume is the Silverhound terminal. You watch the Excel heading left towards an old palace in overgrown gardens. Do you go to the terminal (turn to 179) or follow the Excel (turn to 123)?

383

You walk towards the door and it slides open. You enter and find yourself looking at the back of an administration Android. It senses you and spins around.

ADMIN ANDROID   SKILL 5   STAMINA 6

If you win, turn to 311.

384

As you plough into the water the creatures swarm all around you with their mouths open. *Test your Fear Factor*. If you are frightened, reduce your STAMINA and SKILL by 1 point each. The illusion fades, and you carry on to the north. Turn to 318.

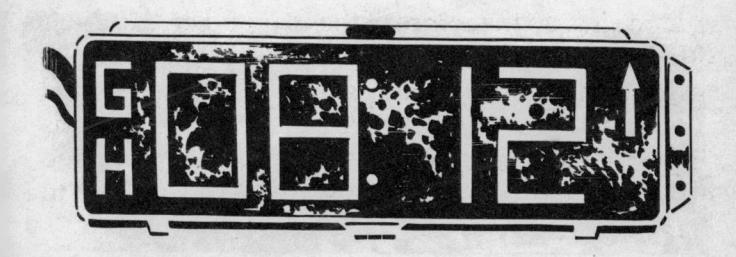

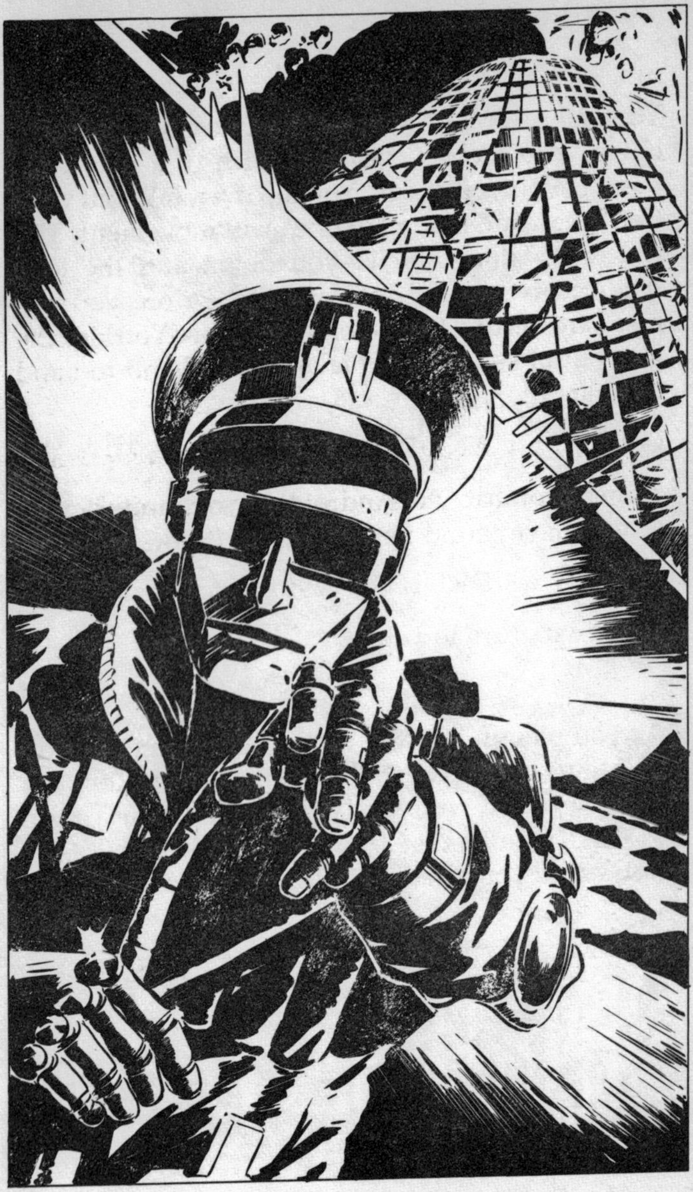

You make a break for cover. The two GromPols give chase. You feel the distinct swish of a stun shot passing your left cheek. You flip over, take out your Catchman and fire, all in one swift movement. The Catchman does not let you down and the lead Android is covered in plasti-net. Before you can reset, the second GromPol is on to you. You kick the gun out of its hand and take it on in hand-to-hand combat.

GROMPOL ANDROID   SKILL 7   STAMINA 10

As in all combat with Androids, if you throw double 6, you have found its weak spot. If you win, turn to 254.

386

Deduct 2 TIME units. You come to and find yourself chained up in a warehouse full of crates marked 'Escargot'. Suddenly someone kicks you from behind. It is a Bandit. He explains that he has sold tickets to all the rogues of Paris who want to see a Tracer fight. You look around and there is quite a crowd up on the crates, placing bets and shouting at one another. He frees you and throws you a pair of spiked steel gloves. You get up and see that your opponent is a typical native of Gigantis 8: he is one and a half times your height, muscle-bound and fearless – the nearest thing to a non-fabricated, ultimate warrior. The Gigantian is also wearing spiked gloves. As he rumbles towards you, you catch sight of a window by the crates. Do you try to break out (turn to **125**) or stay and fight (turn to **115**)?

387

You are in a large room. In the corner there are six Groms, all with snail shells poking out of their ears. They are trying to play a game of chess, but roll about in uncontrollable laughter as each in turn upsets the pieces. You sense something behind you, and you turn around to see a Horned Guard with an arm upraised, about to sink an axe into your head . . .

388

You have no time to set the Catchman, so you have to fight unarmed. Beware: Lurgans are famed for their dirty fighting.

LURGAN   SKILL 9   STAMINA 10

If you lose, turn to **226**. If you win, you head for the ZipCar (turn to **150**).

389

At the bottom there is no light. You hear a creaking and smell burning plastic. Willi limps over to you. It has lost vocal functions and, frankly, you are grateful. Willi lights up its eyes and you look around. You are among what seem to be the foundations of a building. Large vertical metal shafts are sunk into the earth. On one there is a small inspection ladder and Willi motions for you to go up it. You ask why it doesn't come with you and it points at its leg. Will you walk down the tunnel with Willi (turn to **193**) or climb the ladder alone (turn to **25**)?

390

Your memory is perfect and you get to the Ents Complex from a side-street; there, just where it should be, is an inspection cover. You lift the rusty metal with great difficulty and close it behind you. Turn to **114**.

391

You bank right and slow down as you approach a forest. The trees are tall and thin. You weave in between them until the fuel gauge flashes that your tank is almost empty. You stop at a road; there is no sound of pursuit. You hide the bike and stand on the road. Do you go left (turn to **103**) or right (turn to **327**)?

392

You are in Brown room, Level 4. Reduce OXYGEN by 1 unit. There is one door leading up. Turn to **196**.

393

You follow him into the building. It is dark and you hear someone running up a staircase. You follow, but cannot find any trace of him. You go out and stand in the maze of alleyways and buildings. Deduct 2 TIME units and turn to **207**.

394

The water has completely filled the corridor. You must swim underwater from chamber to chamber. Throw two dice and add up the result: this is the distance you must swim to get to the next chamber. Throw one die and add the number to your STAMINA score: this is your ability to swim the distance. If your ability is equal to or greater than the distance, then you've made it. Repeat the procedure three times. If you ever fail, you have to wait till the water subsides, treading water and breathing the stale trapped air: this will take all your remaining TIME units. If you succeed, turn to **96**.

395

Reduce TIME by 2 units. You are in a chamber with exits north-east (turn to **2**), east (turn to **85**) and west (turn to **56**).

396

You leave the shop, without having found anything interesting, and turn the corner into a wider road. You walk along for a time. Turn to **83**.

397

You are in Ochre room, Level 4. Reduce OXYGEN by 1 unit. There is one door leading up. Turn to **215**.

398

The Mark III drops into a forest. The ejectormatic does not work. Your mission fails on impact.

399

You kick out at the first Android and manage to disable it with a blow to the automotive circuits. It falls in the way of a blaster shot from the second GromPol, who you take on in hand-to-hand combat.

GROMPOL ANDROID   SKILL 8   STAMINA 12

If you win, turn to **328**. If you lose, turn to **168**.

400

You have succeeded in your mission. The Galactic President grants you an Iridium AmEx Credit Card. You will not have to go through the dangers and loneliness of the Rogue Tracer lifestyle ever again. Well, at least until you are needed for another special mission, in the wake of the Gromulans' quest for *revenge*!